AAPC CPC Exam Guide

The Certified Professional Coder (CPC) credential is the highest sta[n]dard [...] [physi]cian office settings. Certified CPC professionals help to maintain compliance and profitabili[t]y [within medical practices through accurate] medical coding and documentation.

- 10,000 Series CPT®
- 20,000 Series CPT®
- 30,000 Series CPT®
- 40,000 Series CPT®
- 50,000 Series CPT®
- 60,000 Series CPT®
- Anatomy
- Anesthesia
- Coding Guidelines
- Compliance and Regulatory
- Evaluation and Management
- HCPCS Level II
- ICD-10-CM
- Laboratory/Pathology
- Medical Terminology
- Medicine
- Radiology

CONTENTS

CONTENTS

<u>Answer Key & Rationale</u>

10,000 Series CPT®

1. A 31-year-old male arrives at general surgery for a pilonidal cyst that has been unresponsive to antibiotic therapy at his primary care physician's (PCP) office. There is a large amount of tenderness and edema at the site and the area is erythematic and warm to the touch. The patient's pain has been increasing and, on palpation, the surgeon notes that the cyst is larger than six cm in diameter and appears to be deep. After discussion with the patient, it is decided to perform an incision and drainage (I&D) at the surgeon's office, with \ no sedation other than local use of Lidocaine. The area was prepped and numbed with Lidocaine and an incision was made, allowing a large amount of purulent drainage to be expressed. The area was packed with gauze and the procedure was completed without any complications. The patient will follow up in the office in one week for recheck and is to continue on the antibiotic prescribed by his PCP. Which of the following codes should you use?

    A. 10060
    B. 10061
    C. 10080
    D. 10081

2. A 35-year-old male returns to the general surgeon's office with recurrent episodes of infected pilonidal cysts. He has had the cyst incised and drained (I&D) once at his primary care physician's office and once at the surgeon's office. The last I&D was approximately four months ago. He returns to the office today to discuss further treatment. It is decided that he will undergo outpatient surgery so he can be sedated and the cyst will be excised with the base curetted. During surgery, it was noted that there was an extensive sinus tract. The wound will be packed open, requiring daily dressing changes and he will return to the postop clinic for a recheck in one week. Which of the following codes should you use?

    A. 11771
    B. 11772
    C. 11770
    D. 10080

3. A surgeon is doing a pilonidal cyst incision and drainage with excision in the operating room. What he initially thought was an uncomplicated but deep pilonidal cyst developed into an extensively complicated cyst excision with a z-plasty required to repair the incision. How would you code this procedure?

    A. 11770
    B. 11772
    C. 10081
    D. 11771

4. A 22-year-old male was chopping wood with his friends and accidently slashed his right lower leg with the axe. Upon assessment at the emergency room, it was determined that he had sliced through all layers of skin and the wound was down to muscle, but no arteries were involved. He required layered sutured closure including the deeper layers of subcutaneous tissue, and superficial fascia as well as the epidermis and dermis. His wound was measured at approximately 25 cm. How would you code this procedure?

    A. 12035
    B. 12036
    C. 12045
    D. 12046

5. A 6-year-old boy was bitten by a dog and sustained multiple lacerations as a result. He has a 5 cm laceration on his right lower arm, a 2 cm laceration on his left hand, and a 2.6 cm laceration to the right side of his lower cheek. While in the ER, the

wounds were flushed, then the patient was sedated and the arm and hand lacerations were repaired. Intermediate repair was necessary for the facial laceration due to the depth of the wound and layered closure was performed. The patient was also given a tetanus shot and started on antibiotics. What CPT codes would you use for the laceration repairs of this child and what order is correct?

A. 12002, 12013
B. 12002, 12013 -59
C. 12032, 12002 -59
D. 12032, 12002

6. A 78-year-old male arrives at a dermatology office with multiple skin tags on his arms, neck, and torso. There are a total of 14 lesions that need to be removed and the dermatologist removes all 14 tags within the office. What is the correct code for this procedure?

A. 11101
B. 11200
C. 11201
D. 11300

7. A 60-year-old woman presents to her dermatologists office with a reddish brown lesion on her right upper arm. It is approximately 0.8 cm in diameter and is raised. The patient and provider decide to proceed with a shave excision and will send this to pathology for confirmation. The dermatologist suspects this is a benign angiofibroma. The patient receives local anesthetics at the site and the area is excised with a sharp razor. What is the correct code for this procedure?

A. 11300
B. 11301
C. 11302
D. 11305

8. A 12-year-old boy presents to his pediatrician's office with multiple molluscumcontagiosum on his face, neck and upper right shoulder. They have been present for about 15 months and are getting larger. His parents are concerned about his appearance and that he keeps scratching them. He was treated once for a local infection on his neck, about three months ago. His parents would like to have these removed or be referred to dermatology. The pediatrician discusses options and the parents opt to use cryotherapy with Histofreeze that the pediatrician has in his office. In total, there are six lesions on his right shoulder, eight on his neck and five on his cheek. What CPT code would you use?

A. 17111
B. 17110
C. 17000
D. 17004

9. A 24-year-old woman found a lump in her right breast during a routine exam. She had a mammogram, which confirmed the lump, and then met with a surgeon for a needle biopsy without imaging. What code would you use for this procedure?

A. 19085
B. 19100
C. 19101

D. 19086

10. A 22-year-old female is concerned about her inverted nipples. She would like them to be corrected and sees a plastic surgeon for a consult. She is self-conscious about this issue and wants to fix it. The plastic surgeon explains her options and they decide to correct this complaint. What code would you use for this procedure?

A. 19350
B. 19357
C. 19355
D. 19499

20,000 Series CPT®

1. A patient was suffering from severe hallux valgus of the right foot. The physician excised extraneous bone from the lateral end of the proximal phalanx and the medial eminence of the metatarsal bone. The physician inserted the implant in the lateral end of the proximal phalanx. What is the correct CPT code for this procedure?

A. 28290
B. 28292
C. 28293
D. 28296

2. A 15-year-old boy was pushed during a basketball game and landed face down, hitting the bottom bleacher with his nose. There was immediate swelling and bruising and the nose was displaced to the left. In the ER, the left nasal passage was not patent and the septum was deviated. The patient was taken to the operating room and closed treatment of the nasal fracture with stabilization was performed. Which code is correct for this procedure?

A. 21310
B. 21315
C. 21320
D. 21325

3. A 67-year-old male has an intramuscular tumor of his right scalp over the parietal bone that is approximately 3 cm in diameter. It is getting larger and is causing him pain. He elects to have it removed and will have this excised in the OR as an outpatient procedure. Which procedure code is correct?

A. 21011
B. 21012
C. 21013
D. 21014

4. A 76-year-old woman has noticed a growth along the left side of her neck that is increasing in size. Initially it looked like a mosquito bite, but has increased over the last three months to a dime size, approximately 1.8 cm. Her PCP believes it is a lipoma and sends her to surgery for assessment. It was removed in the office using local anesthesia. Which code is correct?

A. 21550
B. 21555
C. 21552
D. 21556

5. A 25-year-old obese male has had right-sided flank pain for about two months and noticed a lump during work one day. He initially thought it was a muscle spasm and ignored it, but it has increased in size and has gotten more painful. He went through a CT scan, which showed an intramuscular mass consistent to the physical exam that is approximately 6 cm in diameter. Due to the size and presentation, it was decided to excise the tumor. What is the correct code to use for this procedure?

A. 21931
B. 21932
C. 21933
D. 21935

6. A 35-year-old patient has a lipoma on her upper back over her scapula, which causes increased discomfort when her bra strap rubs against it. She has already met with her surgeon and this procedure will be performed in his office because it is only 2.75 cm in diameter and only involves the subcutaneous layer. What CPT code would you use for this procedure?

A. 21920
B. 21930
C. 21931
D. 21932

7. There is a large mass noted on a 56-year-old man's right flank. Due to the size and asymptomatic characteristics, a CT scan was performed and biopsy was recommended. This is a deeply rooted tumor and the patient will be sedated during this procedure. What code should you use for a deep tissue biopsy?

A. 21920
B. 21925
C. 21935
D. 21936

8. A 54-year-old female with degenerative disc disease at L4-L5 undergoes surgical repair with anterior approach for discectomy and fusion to try to prevent further discomfort. What CPT code would you use for this procedure?

A. 22554
B. 22556
C. 22558
D. 22585

9. A 56-year-old man undergoes percutaneous vertebroplasty with vertebral augmentation to L2-L3 with unilateral injection. What is the correct CPT code for this procedure?

A. 22510
B. 22511
C. 22513
D. 22526

10. A 37-year-old woman notices a lump in her left lower abdominal wall. A large, 6 cm tumor was found on CT scan along the musculature of the abdominal wall. This was removed and found to be a desmoid tumor. What is the code for this procedure?

A. 22900
B. 22901
C. 22902
D. 22903

30,000 Series CPT®

1. A physician removed a 54-year-old male's old pulse generator on a dual lead system cardioverter-defibrillator and replaced it with a new one. During the procedure, the surgeon determined that the electrodes needed to be replaced as well and removed the old electrodes, replacing them with new ones. What are the correct codes for this surgical procedure?

A. 33262, 33243 –51, 33249 –51
B. 33263, 33241 –51, 33244 –51
C. 33263, 33243 –51, 33249 –51
D. 33262, 33241 –51, 33249 –51

2. What is the difference between arteriosclerosis and arteriostenosis?

A. –sclerosis is the enlargement of an artery and –stenosis is the narrowing of an artery
B. . –sclerosis is the blocking of an artery and –stenosis is the hardening of an artery
C. –sclerosis is the hardening of an artery and –stenosis is the narrowing of an artery
D. –sclerosis is the enlargement of an artery and –stenosis is the hardening of an artery

3. A physician performed a thromboendarterectomy with a patch graft on the common femoral artery of a 63-year-old female with advanced lower arterial plaque. What is the correct code for this procedure?

A. 35301
B. 35302
C. 35355
D. 35371

4. A 14-year-old patient with an abscessed tooth presented to the physician's office with possible sepsis. The tooth had gone untreated for two weeks, and now the patient is experiencing a high fever, severe headaches and toothaches and malaise and fatigue. The physician suspects that the bacteria from the tooth has spread to the patient's blood and is now a systemic infection. As part of the office procedure, the physician orders a CBC in order to examine the bacterial levels in the patient's blood. After the physician writes the orders, the nurse performs a venipuncture on the patient in order to obtain a blood sample. What is the correct code for the collection of the blood only?

A. 36416
B. 36415
C. 36410
D. 36406

5. A 48-year-old patient was brought to the Emergency Department following a horseback riding injury. The patient was riding in the woods when the horse spooked at the sight of a snake and bucked the patient, who was subsequently kicked by the horse in the abdomen. The patient was suffering severe internal pain, and upon presentation to the ED, the abdomen was stiff and distended. Suspecting an internal splenic injury, the physician ordered emergency surgery. During the surgery, the physician performed a partial lateral splenectomy with a splenorrhaphy on the anterior face of the spleen. Upon gross inspection, the remaining organs were all intact. The physician then sutured the abdominal cavity and admitted the patient to the ICU for observation. What is the correct procedure code for this service?

A. 38115
B. 38101, 38115

C. 38101
D. 38120

6. A physician performed an X-ray of the spleen and portal system. Assign the appropriate CPT code(s).

A. 38200, 75810-26
B. 38200
C. 75810
D. 38200, 75810

7. After careful selection and testing of bone marrow donors, a potential candidate was found for a patient with severe leukemia. The physician collected a small sample of the potential donor's bone marrow via aspiration technique. This sample was then sent to pathology to determine whether or not it would be a match for the patient's bone marrow. What is the correct code for the procedure performed by the physician?

A. 38221
B. 38220
C. 38230
D. 38232

8. A physician performed the open excision of two deep axillary nodes in a 45-year-old female patient. What is the correct code for this procedure?

A. 38500
B. 38555
C. 38525
D. 38525 (X2)

9. A physician performed a lymphangiography with insertion of radioactive tracer for identification of sentinel node. What is the correct code for this procedure?

A. 38790 -50, 75803
B. 38790, 75801
C. 38792 -50, 75803
D. 38792, 75801

10. A physician performed a resection of the diaphragm utilizing an autogenous free muscle flap. What is the correct CPT code?

A. 39561
B. 39560
C. 39540
D. 39541

40,000 Series CPT®

1. A newborn needed a frenectomy, due to a tongue tie, to allow her to breastfeed properly. What CPT code should be used for this procedure?

    A. 40806
    B. 40819
    C. 40820
    D. 40899

2. A 10-year-old involved in a MVA lacerated his posterior tongue. Laceration was 2.4 cm in length. What code should be used for repair of this child's tongue?

    A. 41250
    B. 41251
    C. 41252
    D. 41599

3. A 25-year-old smoker has a lesion on the right anterior portion of his tongue. He needs to have a biopsy done of this lesion. What CPT code should be used for this procedure?

    A. 41100
    B. 41105
    C. 41108
    D. 41112

4. A patient has been having recurrent ulcerations on his uvula. He is scheduled for a biopsy of these ulcerations. What CPT code should be used?

    A. 42000
    B. 42104
    C. 42100
    D. 42140

5. A newborn needs to have a cleft palate repaired. His cleft involves the soft and hard palates only. What CPT code would you use for a palatoplasty for this child?

    A. 42200
    B. 42205
    C. 42210
    D. 42215

6. A 70-year-old woman has an abscess on her soft palate that needs to be drained. She is able to have this procedure done in the ER by otolaryngology. What CPT code should be used?

A. 42000
B. 42100
C. 42104
D. 42140

7. What CPT code should be used for complicated abscess drainage of the parotid gland?

A. 42300
B. 42305
C. 42310
D. 42320

8. A 64-year-old woman has a sublingual salivary cyst that needs to be removed. What CPT code should be used for this procedure?

A. 42400
B. 42405
C. 42408
D. 42409

9. An 8-year-old girl is going to have a tonsillectomy and adenoidectomy for recurrent strep throats. What CPT code should be used for this patient's procedure?

A. 42825
B. 42830
C. 42820
D. 42821

10. A 39-year-old man has been having a recurrent issue, feeling as though there is a lump in his throat. His ENT performed a fiberoptic laryngoscopy on him in the office and it was noted that he had enlarged lingual tonsils. Due to persistent problems and not responding to medication, he is scheduled for lingual tonsil excision. What CPT code should be used for this procedure?

A. 42825
B. 42826
C. 42860
D. 42870

1. A pediatrician performed a routine circumcision on a newborn baby boy in a hospital setting. The physician anesthetized the area with dorsal penile block, clamped the foreskin away from the tip of the penis and excised the excess foreskin. What is the correct code for the circumcision?

A. 54160
B. 54150 -47
C. 54150
D. 54160 -47

2. A physician performed an orchiopexy via an inguinal approach for intra-abdominal testis. What is the correct code for this procedure?

A. 54692
B. 54650
C. 54690
D. 54640

3. A physician performed a bilateral excision of the vas deferens for the purpose of sterilization on a 45-year-male. What is the correct code for this procedure?

A. 55250
B. 55250 -50
C. 55200
D. 55200 -50

4. PROCEDURAL NOTE
PATIENT: Ray, Alexander
AGE: 59
DATE: 02/15/2015
PREOPERATIVE DIAGNOSIS: Prostate Cancer, Primary
POSTOPERATIVE DIAGNOSIS: Same
PROCEDURE: TURP

A patient was placed in supine position on the operating table, draped and anesthetized accordingly. Using a resectoscope with light source, the physician located the prostate and resected the malignant prostatic tissue with electrocautery knife, leaving the appropriate margins. The physician removed the resectoscope and the patient was catheterized for drainage of his bladder contents and resected prostatic tissue. The patient tolerated the procedure well and was transferred to postoperative recovery. What is the correct code for this surgical procedure?

A. 52601 -58
B. 52601
C. 52500
D. 52630

5. A patient with Bartholin's gland cyst presents to the clinic for incision and drainage of the cyst. Due to the size and area of the cyst, the physician decides to incise the cyst and suture the lateral sides, leaving one side open for drainage. Which of the following codes would represent the physician's work?

A. 56420
B. 56740
C. 56440
D. 53060

6. A physician performed a colpopexy with suspension of the vaginal apex via laparoscope. What is the correct code for the procedure?

A. 57280
B. 57282
C. 57283
D. 57425

7. A 36-year-old woman with a history of multiple complicated ectopic pregnancies presented to the clinic for abdominal hysterectomy. Two days ago, an advanced interstitial uterine ectopic pregnancy was discovered and after careful consideration the patient elected to have a full hysterectomy. After the patient was prepped and anesthetized, the obstetrician performed a full incisional hysterectomy with removal of ectopic pregnancy, without removal of ovaries. Patient tolerated the procedure well and was sent to post-operational recovery.

How should the OB code for this surgical procedure?

A. 58150
B. 59120
C. 59135
D. 59136

8. A 23-year old woman, pregnant with her second child, received antepartum care from her physician in Atlanta, GA. After 9 visits with her physician in Atlanta, the patient moved to Albuquerque, NM where she continued her prenatal care with a new doctor. The new physician saw the patient for the remaining antepartum visits. The new physician also performed vaginal delivery and postpartum care, which included the 6-week postpartum checkup. How should the physician in Atlanta code for his services?

A. 59426
B. 59425
C. 59410
D. 59430

9. A woman with polyhydramnios presented to the OB/GYN clinic for amniocentesis with reduction of her amniotic fluid. After prepping the patient with local anesthetic and with ultrasound guidance, the physician inserted the needle with therapeutic drainage system, and drained 18 cc of amniotic fluid from the patient. The needle was then removed under ultrasound guidance and surgical site was monitored for bleeding. The patient tolerated the procedure well and was scheduled to return in one week for another evaluation and possible treatment of her polyhydramnios. What code should be reported for these services?

A. 59000
B. 59001, 76946
C. 59001

D. 59000, 76946

10. A 27-year-old pregnant woman presented to the hospital maternity ward to deliver her third baby. She was 39 weeks pregnant and has had no complications so far. The patient planned on a vaginal delivery. Her oldest child was born vaginally and her second was born via cesarean section. Her OB, who had provided her antepartum care, was able to successfully complete a vaginal delivery with no complications. Her OB also provided postpartum care to the patient. What procedure code should be reported by the OB?

A. 59400
B. 59510
C. 59620
D. 59610

60,000 Series CPT®

1. A young man has to have a lumbar spinal tap performed to obtain cerebrospinal fluid. This will be done with a needle for diagnostic purposes so that the fluid can be tested. What is the correct code for this procedure?

   A. 62269
   B. 62270
   C. 62272
   D. 62273

2. A patient needs to have a lumbar laminectomy without discectomy. Which code is correct for this procedure?

   A. 63001
   B. 63003
   C. 63005
   D. 63011

3. A 40-year-old man needs to have a percutaneous implantation of a neurostimulator electrode array to the trigeminal nerve, which is a cranial nerve. What code is correct for this procedure?

   A. 64550
   B. 64553
   C. 64555
   D. 64561

4. A 62-year-old man needs to have a trigeminal nerve block to help with the pain caused by shingles. What CPT code should be used for this procedure?

   A. 64400
   B. 64402
   C. 64405
   D. 64408

5. During oral surgery, the lingual nerve was transected. What CPT code should be used for this transection?

   A. 64732
   B. 64734
   C. 64740
   D. 64742

6. A 53-year-old woman has been having significant sciatica. She is going to have a neuroplasty of the sciatic nerve. What is the correct code for this procedure?

A. 64702
B. 64704
C. 64708
D. 64712

7. A 26-year-old man who had right ACL reconstruction surgery received a femoral nerve block. What CPT code should be used for the femoral nerve block?

A. 64445
B. 64447
C. 64449
D. 64450

8. A patient needs to have an anesthetic agent injected into the superior hypogastric plexus nerve. What CPT code should be used for this procedure?

A. 64505
B. 64510
C. 64517
D. 64520

9. A 74-year-old man with pancreatic cancer is going to have his celiac plexus nerve destroyed by a neurolytic agent without radiologic monitoring, to help with the intense pain that is caused by his cancer. What is the correct code for this procedure?

A. 64646
B. 64650
C. 64680
D. 64681

10. A middle-age man, who has significant peptic ulcers, is going to have a vagotomy to help reduce stomach acid production. He is going to have the vagus nerve transected using an abdominal approach. What is the correct code for this procedure?

A. 64755
B. 64760
C. 64763
D. 64766

Anatomy

1. A patient is injured in a motor-cross accident and shattered two of his vertebrae. Now he is paralyzed from the chest down and can move his arms, but not his legs. At what level is his injury?

A. Cervical
B. Lumbar
C. Thoracic
D. Sacral

2. The tympanic membrane is often referred to as:

A. A taste bud
B. The ear drum
C. The stirrup
D. The inner ear

3. What is a result of a nasal polyp?

A. It will cause nose cancer in the affected patient
B. It can change the shape of the nose and necessitate rhinoplasty
C. It results in the release of histamine causing an allergic reaction
D. It can obstruct the nasal passageway making it difficult to breathe

4. Which of the following is a type of cyanosis that presents on the fingers and toes and may indicate a need for oxygen therapy for the patient?

A. Central cyanosis
B. Peripheral cyanosis
C. Medial cyanosis
D. Embolytic cyanosis

5. The term "alopecia" is commonly referred to as what?

A. Athlete's foot
B. Hair loss
C. Heat rash
D. Head lice

6. When a doctor manipulates a dislocated joint back into place, he:

A. Reduces the subluxation
B. Manipulates the fracture
C. Suspends the dislocation
D. Reduces the suspension

7. What is the difference between a craniotomy and a craniectomy?

A. A craniectomy removes a part of the skull and allows the surgeon to perform the craniotomy

B. A craniotomy replaces the part of the skull that was removed; a craniectomy does not replace it

C. A craniotomy allows access into the patient's spinal column; a craniectomy is repairs the patient's spinal column

D. There is no difference between the two procedures

8. If a doctor performs only the antepartum portion of a patient's obstetrical care, when did she take care of the patient?

A. Before the patient delivered the baby

B. During the patient's delivery

C. After the patient's delivery

D. Before, during, and after the patient's delivery

9. If a patient is in the prone position, he is:

A. Lying flat on his back

B. Lying flat on his stomach

C. Sitting up straight

D. Lying flat on his back with his feet elevated

10. The superior eyelid is also referred to as the:

A. Lower eyelid

B. Edge of the eyelid that holds the lower lashes

C. The site of the tear duct

D. Upper eyelid

Anesthesia

1. A 17 year-old patient presented to the orthopedist office after having fallen off his skateboard. He suffered a closed fracture to the left tibia and fibula as well as a severe sprain to the right wrist. The patient was in severe pain so an anesthesiologist administered anesthesia to him, while the physician manipulated the fractures back into place and applied the cast to the lower left leg. What are the appropriate anesthesia code(s)?

    A. 01820, 01490
    B. 01462
    C. 01480, 01820
    D. 01490

2. PROCEDURAL NOTE
PATIENT: Lopez, Olga
AGE: 76 years
DATE: 11/05/2014
PATIENT DIAGNOSIS: Multiple skull lymphomas
PROCEDURE: Craniotomy converted to craniectomy of left anterior cranial base
ANESTHESIA: General endotracheal

The patient was placed in supine position on operating table and anesthesia was successfully administered. The patient was then prepped in the usual manner. An incision was made on the midline of the patient's anterior cranial base and the surgeon dissected the epidermal layer to reveal the skull. Three .2 to .4cm lymphomas were then located and the skull bone was excised in one piece to remove the affected areas, leaving .1cm margins. Halfway through the procedure the patient's blood pressure dropped, which was difficult to control for the remainder of the procedure. Due to the patient's drop in blood pressure, the surgeon decided to convert the procedure to a craniectomy, therefore bone grafts were not placed. A drain was placed beneath the remaining skull base and the edges of the skin were then sutured back together using 4-0 vicryl sutures. A sterile dressing was placed on the excision site. The patient was then removed from endotracheal anesthesia and remained under physician supervision until her blood pressure stabilized. She was then taken to the recovery room and scheduled for a bone graft at a later date.

    A. 00210, 99135
    B. 00211, 99100
    C. 00192, 99135, 99100
    D. 00192, 99100

3. When reporting the time involved for an anesthesia procedure when do you start and stop the clock? What is the correct answer?

    A. Time starts when the patient is in the pre-operative waiting area before the anesthesiologist is present and ends at the end of the surgery time.
    B. Time starts when the patient is in the operating room and the anesthesiologist begins to prepare the patient for the induction of the anesthesia and ends in the operating room at the end of the surgery time.
    C. Time starts when the patient is in the operating room and the anesthesiologist begins to prepare the patient for the induction of the anesthesia and ends when the anesthesiologist is no longer in attendance after reporting to the nurses in the PACU (post-anesthesia care unit).
    D. Time starts when the patient is in the operating room before the anesthesiologist is in attendance and ends in the PACU after the anesthesiologist gives report to the post-anesthesia care unit nurses.

4. It is possible to have more than one qualifying circumstances for an anesthesia code. What qualifying circumstance codes should be added onto the procedure code for lower abdominal hernia repair in a child younger than one year of age who became significantly hypotensive during the procedure, causing an emergency condition?

A. 00834, 99100, 99135
B. 00834, 99100, 99140
C. 00834, 99140, 99135
D. 00834, 99140

5. A 54-year-old man is having a coronary artery bypass grafting with pump oxygenator where the anesthesiologist is also using total body hypothermia. What is the correct code for this procedure?

A. 00566, 99116
B. 00566, 99135
C. 00567, 99116
D. 00567, 99135

6. A physician harvested a viable left cornea, liver, and heart from a declared brain-dead patient. What anesthesia services should have been provided?

A. 01990
B. No anesthesia services should have been performed on a brain-dead patient
C. 33930, 47133-51, 65110-51
D. 01990-P6

7. A physician performed a total hip arthroplasty and an excision of a patellar bone spur. Code for the anesthesia services only.

A. 01400, 01214
B. 01380, 01400
C. 01214
D. 01215, 01400

8. A physician performed burn debridement on a 75-year-old male, who sustained third degree burns over 13% of his body, while burning dead brush in his back yard. Code for the anesthesia services only.

A. 01951, 01952, 01953
B. 01951, 01953 (X2), 99100
C. 01952, 01953, 99100
D. 01952, 01953 (X2)

9. A 38-year-old female patient presented to the office for an extended ophthalmoscopy with retinal drawing. The physician also performed interpretation and report of the findings. The physician performing the procedure also performed the anesthesia service for the patient, due to the fact that the anesthesiologist was not available. What are the correct codes for the procedure?

A. 00148-47
B. 92225-47
C. 92225, 00148-47
D. 92225-47, 00148

10. A 48 year-old-man suffered internal injuries as well as multiple lower body fractures in a multiple-car accident, and presented in an extremely emergent situation. The patient's liver sustained damage and was hemorrhaging. Surgery began immediately, as the patient was not expected to survive without immediate surgery. During the surgery, the orthopedic surgeon manipulated the patient's tibia fracture and set the bone with a percutaneous fixation. Code for the anesthesia services only.

A. 01462, 00794-P4
B. 01462, 00792
C. 00792-P5
D. 00792-P5, 01462

Coding Guidelines

1. Mr. Jones was examined after a car accident as a requirement of his car insurance claim. Which modifier is appropriate to use on the claim?

A. -22
B. -51
C. -99
D. -32

2. A physician performed a complex repair of the scalp measuring 7.2 cm and an intermediate repair of the arm measuring 3.4 cm. The repairs are different complexities, so they would be reported with separate repair codes, but you would need to add a modifier to indicate that they are two separate procedures performed on the same date of service. Which modifier would you use?

A. -59
B. -51
C. -25
D. -24

3. A 32-year-old woman with repeat urinary tract infections presented to the office with painful urination. Suspecting another UTI, the physician sent a urine sample to the lab to identify the bacteria causing the infection. The physician's office billed for the laboratory service themselves, even though they sent the sample to an outside lab for the test. What modifier is appropriate in this case?

A. Modifier -99
B. Modifier -90
C. Modifier -52
D. No modifier would be necessary

4. What are the two most common modifiers used in radiological services?

A. -51 and -26
B. - TC and -26
C. S&I and -26
D. - TC and -51

5. What organizations make up the "Cooperating Parties" for the ICD-10-CM guidelines and who approved these guidelines?

A. American Hospital Association (AHA), American Health Information Management Association (AHIMA), National Center for Health Statistics (NCHS), U.S. Federal Government's Department of Health and Human Services (DHHS)

B. American Hospital Association (AHA), National Center for Health Statistics (NCHS), World Health Organization (WHO), U.S. Federal Government's Department of Health and Human Services (DHHS)

C. American Hospital Association (AHA), American Health Information Management Association (AHIMA), Centers for Medicare & Medicaid Services (CMS), National Center for Health Statistics (NCHS)

D. American Health Information Management Association (AHIMA), Centers for Medicare & Medicaid Services (CMS), National Center for Health Statistics (NCHS), World Health Organization (WHO)

6. How do you locate a code in the ICD-10-CM?

A. Locate it in the Alphabetic Index then verify it in the Tabular List and then submit it to insurance.
B. Locate it in the Alphabetic Index and then submit it to insurance. There is no need to use the Tabular List.
C. Locate it in the Tabular List and submit to insurance. There is no need to use the Alphabetic Index.
D. There is no need to use either the Alphabetic Index or the Tabular List to identify the ICD-10-CM code.

7. Can you specify laterality in the ICD-10-CM codes?

A. No, you cannot specify laterality with the ICD-10-CM.
B. Yes, you can specify laterality for some codes. Some codes do not have "bilateral" listed, so in this case the code for "right" and "left" would be assigned.
C. Yes, you can specify laterality in the ICD-10-CM codes when the side is not mentioned in the medical record.
D. No, you cannot specify laterality even if it is mentioned in the medical record when using the ICD-10-CM codes.

8. Can you use signs, symptoms or unspecified codes in the ICD-10-CM instead of an actual diagnosis?

A. Yes, symptom/sign codes can be used, but there are no unspecified codes in the ICD-10-CM
B. No, in ICD-10-CM the purpose of added codes is to prevent the use of signs, symptoms or unspecified codes
C. Yes, if a definitive diagnosis hasn't been made by the end of the patient encounter, then unspecified codes or sign/symptom codes may be used to best describe the diagnosis at the end of the encounter
D. No, ICD-10-CM doesn't even have unspecified codes as an option

9. What is sequela or "late effects" in the ICD-10-CM coding guidelines?

A. It is the acute injury or illness right after it has happened
B. It is considered to be the one-month timeframe after an acute injury or illness
C. Sequela is considered to be the effect after the acute phase of the illness or injury within three months of the initial episode
D. Sequela is considered to be the residual effect after the acute phase of the injury or illness without a time limit imposed on it

10. The respiratory system subsection in the CPT manual contains, but is not limited to procedure codes for the following body areas:

A. Nose, mouth, and throat
B. Nose, accessory sinuses, and trachea/bronchi
C. Accessory sinuses, mouth, and stomach
D. Lungs, pleura, and heart

Compliance and Regulatory

1. What does HIPAA stand for?

A. Health Insurance Portability and Accountability Act
B. Health Insurance Protection and Accountability Association
C. Health Insurance Post-Payment Auditing Association
D. Health Insurance Accountability and Auditing Act

2. What is the purpose of provider credentialing?

A. To make sure that your provider is performing the correct procedures
B. To make sure that your provider is correctly licensed to perform procedures
C. To make sure your provider pays all the necessary fees to practice medicine
D. To allow your doctor to check the credentials of private insurance companies

3. In the RBRVS calculation, the GPCI takes into account:

A. The geographic location of a practice or provider
B. The type of provider specialty
C. The malpractice risk of a procedure
D. The overhead cost of the practice

4. What are the correct steps to coding for the best payment outcome?

A. Identify the reason for the encounter based on what the physician documented as the diagnosis without reviewing the medical record. Find the diagnosis in the Tabular List and choose the code with the highest specificity. Assign the code and submit to insurance.
B. Identify the reason for the encounter based on the diagnosed reason and confirmation within the medical record. Find the diagnosis in the Tabular List, confirm it in the Alphabetic Index, assign the code without regard to the specificity and submit to insurance.
C. Identify the reason for the encounter based on the diagnosed reason and confirmation within the medical record. Find the diagnosis in the Alphabetic Index, review entries for modifiers, choose the best code and locate it in the Tabular List, then determine whether the code is the highest level of specificity. If so, assign that code to the encounter. Sequencing is very important, so review this prior to final billing submission.
D. Identify the reason for the encounter based on what the physician documented as the diagnosis after reviewing the medical record. Find the diagnosis in the Alphabetic Index, find it in the Tabular List, and use the first code available without regard to modifiers or specificity.

5. What are Medically Unlikely Edits (MUEs)?

A. Units of service edits created by CMS to lower the Medicare Fee-For-Service paid claims error rate
B. Codes that cannot be reported together because they are mutually exclusive of each other
C. "Add-on" codes that describe a service that can only be reported with another service listed as the primary code
D. Misuse of column two codes with column one codes
6. What does "place of service" reporting refer to?

A. It refers to the location of the billing department, whether in a hospital or physician's office or independent.

B. It refers to the primary location of the provider seeing the patient. If the provider is an outpatient physician, but sees the patient inside the hospital, then the place of service is the outpatient physician's office.

C. Only services in the hospital or in the providers' office are considered "place of service" for reporting purposes.

D. It refers to the location of the setting in which the patient is treated.

7. What is special about services provided in a patient's home?

A. When services are provided in the home by a physician or provider who is not part of an agency, this is considered "non-facility" services

B. When services are provided by a provider or physician who is part of an agency, such as home health, then the service is considered to be provided within a facility

C. Answers A and B are both correct about in home patient care services

D. None of the above options are correct about patient care within the home

8. True or false: Only physicians can use place of service reporting in the CPT guidelines.

A. True, only physicians are considered to be able to provide services to patients.

B. False, the words "physician," "qualified healthcare professional," or "individual" can all be used and even other entities may report the service.

C. False, the term "physician" encompasses all healthcare providers whether registered nurses, physician assistants or nurse practitioners. These terms leave out physical therapists, speech therapists, occupational therapists and other entities that may provide necessary services for the patient.

D. True, only physicians can provide facility and non-facility services and code for them.

9. What is the Federal Anti-Kickback Law and Regulatory Safe Harbors?

A. It protects patients and federal healthcare programs from fraud and abuse by stopping the corrupting influence of money on healthcare decisions. It states that anyone who knowingly and willfully receives or pays anything of value to influence the referral of federal healthcare program business can be held accountable for a felony.

B. It allows physicians to accept money for referrals to certain providers or services for patients within a federal healthcare program.

C. It protects physicians from being charged with a felony if they willfully receive or pay anything of value to influence their medical decisions and best plan of care for the patient.

D. It protects patients, part of federal healthcare programs, from being referred to other providers that aren't in the best interest of the patient.

10. The National Correct Coding Initiative (NCCI) promotes correct coding of healthcare services and prevents payment for incorrectly coded services. There are tables present for these edits to the coding. How often are these edits updated at the Centers for Medicare & Medicaid Services (CMS)?

A. Monthly

B. Quarterly

C. Semi-annually

D.Annually

Evaluation and Management

1. A pediatric patient with a history of asthma and pneumonia presented to the office with severe respiratory distress. The pediatrician performed a detailed history and comprehensive examination, and diagnosed the patient with status asthmaticus. A pulse oxygen level was taken and it was determined that the patient's blood oxygen level was at 88%. The patient was started on a nebulizer treatment at 0950 hours, which lasted until 1015 hours. The physician then re-checked the patient and determined that the patient's breathing had only slightly improved. A pulse oxygen level was taken again and it was determined that the patient was at 92%. The physician then ordered another nebulizer treatment, which was started at 1032 and continued until 1054. After this second breathing treatment, an additional pulse oxygen level was taken and the patient's blood oxygen level had risen to 97%. The pediatrician then determined that the patient needed to be sent for chest x-rays to determine whether or not pneumonia was present in the lungs. Due to the resulting amount of data and risk, the pediatrician considered the MDM of high complexity. The total time spent with the patient was 1 hour 45 minutes.

What E&M codes would you use to code for the office visit?

A. 99214, 99354, 99355 (X2)
B. 99215, 99354, 99355
C. 99215, 99355 (X3)
D. 99215, 99354, 99355 (X2)

2. If a physician performed a female pelvic examination under general anesthesia, you should code for the procedure using an appropriate code from the female genital system subsection of the surgery chapter of the CPT manual. If the physician performed a pelvic examination without general anesthesia, from what chapter or subsection of the CPT manual should you code?

A. Anesthesia
B. Maternity Care and Delivery
C. Evaluation and Management
D. Female Genital

3. A 32-year-old married female presents to her OB/GYN office for diaphragm fitting. After performing a pelvic examination and routine physical, the OB measures the cervix and adjusts the diaphragm so that it fits neatly over the cervical opening. The OB then instructs the patient in how to place the diaphragm for most effective birth control, as well as how to remove, clean, and store the diaphragm. Satisfied that the patient understands how to use the device properly, she allows the patient to leave the office with a follow-up appointment scheduled in one month. How should the OB/GYN code for this visit?

A. 99395
B. 99395, 57170-59
C. 57170
D. 99395, 57170

4. The physician performed an annual examination on a 47-year-old male new patient with a history of congenital heart disease. What is the correct E&M code?

A. 99387
B. 99386
C. 99396
D. 99397

5. The nurse practitioner returned a phone call from a concerned daughter regarding her ailing mother's health. She spent 20 minutes counseling the daughter on how to provide hospice care during the last stages of her mother's life. It had been three weeks since the patient had been seen in the office, and her next scheduled appointment was in two weeks. What E&M service can be reported for this phone call?

A. You cannot report an E&M service for this phone call
B. 99442
C. 98967
D. 99443

6. A patient is admitted to the hospital for observation for possible dehydration. A detailed history is performed with a detailed examination of the patient on the unit. The medical decision making was low complexity and straightforward, so the physician was only on the unit for about 20 minutes. What is the best code to be used for this observation patient?

A. 99218
B. 99219
C. 99220
D. 99224

7. A patient is admitted to the telemetry unit for observation for chest pain, directly from his physician's office. The hospitalist spent a little more than 50 minutes on the unit after the patient arrived, performing a comprehensive examination and obtaining a comprehensive history on the patient. The hospitalist performed moderate complexity medical decision making when ordering labs, telemetry, stress testing and echocardiogram. What is the appropriate code for initial observation care of this patient?

A. 99218
B. 99219
C. 99220
D. 99224

8. A patient admitted in the afternoon for 24-hour observation, after complaining about chest pain in his PCP's office, has worsened during the evening. He now has increasing chest pain, requiring medication for relief; his EKG has changed from his PCP's office; and he is being prepped for a cardiac catheterization because his labs are returning indicating an acute MI. What is the appropriate code for a patient who is unstable after initial observation?

A. 99220
B. 99224
C. 99225
D. 99226

9. A patient admitted to the hospital three days ago is getting ready to be discharged this morning. The attending physician spent more than 30 minutes arranging home health services and talking with the patient and family regarding outpatient rehabilitation and care after right hip replacement. What code should be used for the discharge day management of this patient?

A. 99235
B. 99236
C. 99238

D. 99239

10. A 54-year-old woman is being set up for consultation with general surgery for follow up after a large lump was identified on mammography by the woman's PCP. This office consultation will include a comprehensive history, a comprehensive examination, and moderate-complexity medical decision making because it will involve discussing options, additional tests, and surgery. The surgeon allowed for a 60-minute visit with this woman and her family. What is the appropriate code for consultation?

A. 99242
B. 99243
C. 99244
D. 99245

HCPCS Level II

1. HCPCS Level II codes are updated every quarter by:

A. CMS
B. Medicaid
C. Tricare
D. Commercial payers

2. Appendix 1 in the HCPCS Level II manual contains:

A. An alphabetized list of HCPCS modifiers
B. A table of drugs
C. A list of changes, additions, and deletions
D. A short list of CPT codes to use with HCPCS codes

3. What is the purpose of temporary national codes in the HCPCS Level II manual?

A. They are for procedures that are considered temporary
B. There are no temporary codes, only permanent codes
C. They allow the establishment of codes prior to the January 1st annual update
D. They allow the deletion of codes prior to the January 1st annual update

4. A preoperative patient needs to have an antibiotic started before his operation. He is given 500 mg Ceftriaxone sodium through his IV. What is the correct HCPCS code for this medication?

A. J0715
B. J0696
C. J0696 x2
D. J0697

5. The HCPCS Level II modifier -E1 stands for:

A. Lower Right, Eyelid
B. Upper Right, Eyelid
C. Upper Left, Eyelid
D. Right Hand, Thumb

6. The HCPCS manual includes codes for:

A. Procedures that are also found in the CPT coding manual
B. Supplies, services, and procedures that are not found in the CPT manual
C. Only supplies that you cannot find in the CPT manual
D. All services performed in the office, except for procedures

7. What types of codes are located in the V0000 through V5999 section of the HCPCS manual?

A. Pathology and Laboratory Services
B. Vision and Hearing Services
C. Dental Procedures
D. Transportation Services

8. Which of the following is the best, most effective way to locate the correct code for a service or supply in the HCPCS manual?

A. Look in the Index for the name of the service or supply, and it will direct you to the correct code or range of codes
B. Go directly to Appendix 1 to check the name of the supply, and then find out the route of administration
C. Flip through the sections of the book until you find the correct service or supply and then assign the best code
D. Go directly to the code in the book, and assign the code that looks right

9. HCPCS J-Codes are used to represent:

A. Drugs administered by methods other than the oral method
B. Durable medical equipment
C. Dental procedures not found in the CPT manual
D. Temporary national codes for Medicare

10. When using the table of drugs in the HCPCS Level II manual, you must know the drug's administration route. The abbreviation "VAR" stands for which of the following?

A. Various Routes
B. Variable Routes
C. A Variety of Routes
D. None of the Above

ICD-10-CM

1. A patient with HIV is admitted for enterocolitis due to Clostridium difficile. What is the correct ICD-10-CM code(s) and what is the correct sequence?

A. B20, A04.7
B. B20, A09
C. A04.7, B20
D. A04.7, R75

2. A patient with acute lymphoblastic leukemia is currently undergoing chemotherapy and radiation therapy and develops anemia as a result. He requires admission and a blood transfusion because of this complication caused by the chemotherapy. What ICD-10-CM codes should be used and what is the correct sequence?

A. C91.10, D64.81, T45.1X5A
B. C91.00, T45.1X5A, D64.81
C. D64.81, C91.00, T45.1X5A
D. T45.1X5A, D64.81, C91.00

3. A 35-year-old male with type 1 diabetes, who has an insulin pump, also has diabetic retinopathy without macular edema. He is admitted to the hospital with ketoacidosis without coma. What are the correct ICD-10-CM codes and what is the correct sequence?

A. E10.10, E10.319, Z79.4
B. E10.11, E10.319
C. E10.10, E10.311, Z79.4
D. E10.11, E10.311

4. A 33-year-old woman follows up with her psychiatrist for ongoing major depressive disorder that is considered moderate. She is on a daily medication for this disorder. She also follows up with him for generalized anxiety disorder. She smokes 1.5 packs of cigarettes per day and she reports that this helps her anxiety and, when she doesn't smoke, her anxiety increases. What ICD-10-CM codes are correct and what sequence should they be listed?

A. F33.0, F41.9, F17.200
B. F33.1, F41.1, F17.210
C. F33.0, F41.1, F17.200
D. F33.1, F41.9, F17.210

5. A 21-year-old patient with chronic tension-type headaches that are not intractable relies on daily prophylactic medications to help relieve the headaches. What is the correct ICD-10-CM code for this type of headache?

A. G43.10
B. G44.019
C. G44.201
D. G44.229

6. A 45-year-old patient has a chalazion of her right upper eyelid. What is the correct ICD-10-CM code indicating laterality for this patient?

A. H00.11
B. H00.12
C. H00.13
D. H00.14

7. A 2-year-old patient is here for initial examination and is found to have a right acute serous otitis media and impacted cerumen of the left ear. What are the correct ICD-10-CM codes for this patient in the correct sequence?

A. H65.02, H65.21
B. H61.22, H65.01
C. H65.01, H61.22
D. H65.03, H61.21

8. A patient with a history of asthma is seen in the office for an acute nasopharyngitis (common cold) and increasing difficulty breathing, even using her albuterol inhaler at home 2-3 times a day. She is diagnosed with a common cold and mild intermittent asthma with acute exacerbation. What is the correct sequence of ICD-10-CM codes for this patient?

A. J45.21, J22
B. J45.20, J00
C. J45.31, J00
D. J45.21, J00

9. A 26-year-old man has been diagnosed with Crohn's disease of the large and small intestine without complications. What is the correct ICD-10-CM code for this diagnosis?

A. K50.0
B. K50.1
C. K50.8
D. K50.9

10. An elementary school student who wrestles has been diagnosed with non-bullous impetigo. What is the correct ICD-10-CM code for this type of infectious skin disease?

A. L01.00
B. L01.01
C. L01.02
D. L01.03

Laboratory/Pathology

1. The surgical pathologist obtained three skin tags samples from in the patient's right axilla, as well as four samples of breast tissue from the surgical session. The surgical procedure was a radical bilateral mastectomy, including excision of regional lymph nodes and surrounding tissue. How should the surgical pathologist code for this service?

A. 88304 (X7)
B. 88304 (X3), 88307 (X4)
C. 88305 (X3), 88307 (X4)
D. 88304 (X3), 88309 (X4)

2. A comprehensive metabolic panel and a general health panel is ordered and performed on a patient. What is the correct CPT coding for these laboratory orders?

A. 80053, 80050
B. 80050
C. 80050, 80051
D. 80050, 80048

3. A 26 year old must have a drug screen performed in order to obtain a job at a local nursing home. The nursing home orders a 7-panel drug screen for amphetamines, benzodiazepines, cocaine, heroin, methadone, opiates, and oxycodone. If any of these come up positive by direct optical observation, then definitive drug testing is ordered as reflex testing. This patient did not have any positives on optical observation so no additional testing was performed. What is the correct CPT code for this drug screen?

A. 80300
B. 80301
C. 80302
D. 80303

4. A patient who has been on Digoxin needs to have labs drawn to verify his response to the medication. A total Digoxin level is ordered. What is the correct CPT code for this test?

A. 80162
B. 80163
C. 80159
D. 80178

5. A patient is on two medications needing monitoring. She needs to have a free and total phenytoin drug assay performed. She also needs to have a Topiramate drug assay performed. What are the correct CPT codes for these tests?

A. 80184, 80185, 80201
B. 80183, 80184, 80185
C. 80185, 80186, 80201
D. 80185, 80186,   80200

Medical Terminology

1. This organ is a five-inch tube located behind the mouth that helps close the nasopharynx and larynx when swallowing food. This organ keeps your food out of your respiratory tract and in your digestive tract. What is it called?

A. Esophagus
B. Pharynx
C. Nasopharynx
D. Trachea

2. This condition occurs when the lining of the esophagus becomes inflamed. It is generally caused by an infection or irritation of the esophagus. What is the name of this condition?

A. Esophagitis
B. Barrett's Esophagus
C. Esophageal Varices
D. Mallory-Weiss Tear

3. A dilated and enlarged varicose vein that developed inside the rectum and slipped outside of the anus is called a what?

A. External Hemorrhoid
B. Internal Hemorrhoid
C. Prolapsed Hemorrhoid
D. Varicose Hemorrhoid

4. Within the male genital system, the pair of tubular glands located above the prostate and behind the bladder that lubricate the duct system, nourish the sperm, and contribute fluid to the ejaculate are called:

A. Seminal Vesicles
B. Testes
C. Vas Deferens
D. Epididymis

5. One of the most common prostatic disorders is _____, which is an enlargement of the prostate gland. This disorder may require a transurethral resection of the prostate (TURP).

A. Lower Urinary Tract Symptoms (LUTS)
B. Benign Prostatic Hyperplasia (BPH)
C. Elevated Prostate Specific Antigen (PSA)
D. Prostatic Intraepithelial Neoplasia III (PIN III)

Medicine

1. A 58-year-old patient with decreased hearing decided to undergo bilateral cochlear device implantation in order to restore the gradual decline of his hearing, and prevent total deafness. Due to the position of the device and the size of the patient's mastoid bone that was partially occluding the patient's inner ear, the physician performed a modified mastoidectomy. A mastoidectomy was necessary for the completion of the cochlear device implantation procedure. The physician used an operating microscope throughout the cochlear implantation. How would you code for the procedure?

A. 69930, 69505, 69990
B. 69930, 69501, 69900
C. 69930
D. 69930-50, 69900

2. A patient with a suspected cardiac arrhythmia was given a routine rhythm EKG with three leads in the cardiologist's office. The results of the EKG were sent to the patient's primary care physician, who interpreted the results and determined that the patient's arrhythmia was mild. What is the correct code for the cardiologist's office service only?

A. 93040
B. 93042
C. 93041
D. 93000

3. Mr. Johnson was seen in his primary care physician's office today for an evaluation of chest pains. He has been experiencing shortness of breath as well as intermittent chest pains for the past week. He has also been experiencing tingling and numbness in his left hand and fingers. His primary care physician suspects a cardiac rhythm abnormality and performs a rhythm electrocardiogram in the office. After reading the ECG report, Mr. Johnson's physician determines that his heart rhythm needs more evaluation and refers him to a cardiac specialist. How should the electrocardiogram code be reported?

A. 93000
B. 93010
C. 93042
D. 93040

4. The patient has a dual-chamber pacemaker and was recently seen by his physician for analysis and report of his implanted device. During the visit, the physician connected the system, evaluated its performance, and then disconnected it. What is the correct code for this service?

A. 33213
B. 93289
C. 33208
D. 93288

5. The physician performed a right and left heart catheterization with a left ventriculography on 58-year-old male patient. During catheterization, the patient participated in a physiologic exercise study in the form of a bicycle ergometry. How should you code for this service?

A. 93531, 93464

B. 93451, 93452, 93464
C. 93453, 93464
D. 93453

Radiology

1. A pregnant woman needs to have a fetal echocardiogram performed. This will be done in real time with image documentation (2D) with M-mode recording. What is the correct code for this procedure?

A. 76820
B. 76825
C. 76826
D. 76827

2. A patient needs to have an epidural and, due to compressed discs, this procedure is done under fluoroscopic guidance. What is the correct code for this type of fluoroscopic procedure?

A. 77002
B. 77003
C. 77011
D. 77012

3. A patient undergoes magnetic resonance guidance for needle placement for placement of a localization device. What is the correct code for this procedure?

A. 77011
B. 77012
C. 77021
D. 77022

4. A physician orders a fluoroscopic guidance for needle placement to aspirate a small, possibly malignant lesion on a patient's liver. What is the code for this type of radiologic guidance procedure?

A. 77001
B. 77002
C. 77003
D. 77011

5. A 56-year-old woman is undergoing a bilateral screening mammogram. What is the correct code for this procedure where there is computer-aided detection?

A. 77054
B. 77056
C. 77057
D. 77057, 77052

Answer Key & Rationale

10,000 Series CPT®

1. Answer: C – 10080 is correct because this was a straightforward I&D of a pilonidal cyst. There were no complications mentioned during the procedure. Code s10060 and 10061 are incorrect because they are used for I&Ds of abscesses, but are not specific to pilonidal cysts. Code 10081 is incorrect because it is for a complicated I&D of a pilonidal cyst and the scenario specified that this was an uncomplicated procedure.

2. Answer: A – 11771 is correct for an extensive procedure because it involved excising the cyst and curetting it. Code 11772 is not correct because, while extensive, the excision was not complicated. A complicated excision may include removal down to the sacral fascia or using the surgical technique called marsupialization. Code 11770 is incorrect because this pilonidal cyst was more complicated and was not just a simple pilonidal cyst. Code 10080 is incorrect because this was a complicated pilonidal cyst and it required more than just an I&D because it was also excised.

3. Answer: B – 11772 is correct for this extensively complicated cyst excision requiring a z-plasty closure. Code 11770 is incorrect because this was not a simple pilonidal cyst and it was found to have extensions. Code 10081 is incorrect because, although it is a complicated cyst, it is also being excised and closed. Code 11771 is incorrect because while extensive, this cyst was excised and repaired and also required a complicated excision and closure.

4. Answer: B – 12036 is correct because this wound is considered an intermediate repair due to the multiple layer closure. Also, the wound size was 25 cm on the lower leg. Code 12035 is incorrect because, although it is the correct location, the size is too small. Codes 12045 and 12046 are incorrect because the location is not correct.

5. Answer: C – Code 12032 is being used as the primary procedure code because this code is for 2.6–5 cm facial lacerations and was considered an intermediate repair. The total length of laceration for the arm and hand lacerations was 7 cm, so 12002 is also correct. Because this was for a simple repair that is less complicated than the other repair, it is listed as the secondary procedure code. Modifier -59 is used because there was more than one classification of wounds repaired on this patient. Code 12002 is correct but must be listed as the second code due to it being the less complicated repair. Code 12013 is incorrect because this code is for simple repair of a wound 2.6 cm to 5.0 cm in length and the length of the simple repairs was a total of 7 cm. This code is also specific to the face, ears, eyelids, nose, lips and/or mucous membranes.

6. Answer: B – 11200 is correct because this code can be used for the removal of up to and including 15 skin tags. Code 11101 is incorrect because these are skin tags that are being removed and no biopsy was performed. Code 11201 is incorrect because this is an "add-on" code for each additional 10 lesions after the initial 15. 11300 is incorrect because there was no mention of a shaving being performed.

7. Answer: B – 11301 is correct because this lesion was removed by shaving. It is also 0.6 to 1.0 cm in diameter and is located on the arm. Code 11300 is incorrect because this code is for 0.5 cm diameter lesions or smaller and this patient's lesion is 0.8 cm. Code 11302 is incorrect because this code is used for longer than 1.1 cm to 2 cm diameter lesions. Code 11305 is incorrect because the lesion location is wrong for this code and it is longer than this code indicates.

8. Answer: A – 17111 is correct because he has a total of 19 lesions that were frozen in the pediatrician's office. This code is for destruction of 15+ lesions. Code 17110 is incorrect because this code is for up to 14 lesions such as warts, molluscum, or milia. Codes 17000 and 17004 are both incorrect because they are for actinic keratosis which is not what this little boy was being treated for.

9. Answer: B - 19100 is correct because the needle biopsy was completed without imaging guidance. Codes 19085 and 19086 are incorrect because these involve biopsy with breast localization device placement. Code 19101 is incorrect because this was done through needle biopsy and not an open incisional biopsy.

10. Answer: C - 19355 is for correction of inverted nipples. Code 19350 is incorrect because, although it is listed as nipple/areola reconstruction, there is a specific code for correction of inverted nipples. Code 19357 is incorrect because there was no reconstruction with tissue expander. Code 19499 is incorrect because there is a specific procedure code for this issue.

11-6-20 100%
3-27-21 90%

1. Answer: C – The correct CPT code for this procedure is 28293 (Correction, Hallux Valgus, with or without Sesamoidectomy; Resection of Joint with Implant). Code 28290 is only used for a simple resection without implant. Code 28292 is used for the removal of the lateral end of the proximal phalanx and the medial eminence of the metatarsal bone, but it does not include the implant.

2. Answer: C – 21320 is correct for a closed treatment of the nasal fracture with stabilization. Code 21310 is incorrect because this was treatment without manipulation and code 21315 is incorrect because this was treatment without stabilization. Code 21325 is incorrect because this code is for the open treatment of a nasal fracture.

3. Answer: D – 21014 is correct for excision of a soft tissue tumor of the scalp that is 3 cm. Codes 21011 and 21012 are incorrect because they involve subcutaneous tumors of the face or scalp. Code 21012 is incorrect because this tumor is larger than 2 cm.

4. Answer: B – 21555 is correct for an excision of a subcutaneous lesion smaller than 3 cm of the neck. Code 21550 is incorrect because this code is for a biopsy. Codes 21552 and 21556 are incorrect because of the size and type of tumor present.

5. Answer: C – 21933 is correct for the excision of a tumor that is 6 cm and is an intramuscular tumor. Code 21931 is incorrect because although the size is correct, this is not a subcutaneous tumor. Code 21932 is incorrect because the size is too small and 21935 is incorrect because this did not involve a radical resection.

6. Answer: B – 21930 is the correct code for a subcutaneous soft tissue tumor excision of less than 3 cm. Code 21920 is incorrect because this was a removal and not just a biopsy of the tumor. Code 21931 is incorrect because of the size and 21932 is incorrect because this is not an intramuscular tumor.

7. Answer: B– 21925 is correct for a deep tissue biopsy of the flank mass. Code 21920 is not correct because this wasn't a superficial tissue biopsy. Codes 21935 and 21936 are incorrect because these codes both involve a radical resection of the tumor.

8. Answer: C – 22558 is the only lumbar code listed for anterior lumbar fusion and discectomy. Code 22554 is incorrect because this is the code for cervical arthrodesis. Code 22556 is incorrect because this code is for thoracic discectomy and 22585 is incorrect because this is an "add-on" code for each additional interspace procedure performed, but there was only one performed on this patient.

9. Answer: B – 22511is correct because it is for a lumbosacral percutaneous vertebroplasty of one vertebral body. Code 22510 is incorrect because is it for the cervicothoracic area. Code 22513 is incorrect because is more invasive, including cavity creation and mechanical device. Code 22526 is incorrect because it is the code for a percutaneous intradiscalelectrothermalannuloplasty

10. Answer: B – 22901 is correct because this tumor was 6 cm. Code 22900 is incorrect because the size is larger than 5 cm. Codes 22902 and 22903 are incorrect because they involve a subcutaneous tumor, but this tumor is in the muscle of the abdominal wall.

12-16-20 70%
3-27-21 70%

1. Answer: C – The correct codes for the surgical procedure are 33243 (Removal and Replacement of the Pulse Generator of a Dual Lead System). Code 33243 needs to be included on the claim to indicate the removal of the dual chamber electrodes. The last code that needs to be included on the claim is 33249 (Replacement of the Dual Chamber Electrodes). The last two codes for the service, 33243 and 33249, need to be appended with modifier –51 to indicate that there were multiple procedures performed on the same date of service.

2. Answer: C – The difference between arteriosclerosis and arteriostenosis is that –sclerosis is the hardening of an artery and –stenosis is the narrowing of an artery. Both are conditions of the arteries, which may cause myocardial infarctions or other vascular problems. Diagnosis of either condition can be confirmed via cardiac catheterization procedures. These procedures are located in the surgery and medicine chapters of the CPT manual.

3. Answer: D – The correct code for this procedure is 35371 (Thromboendarterectomy, including Patch Graft, if Performed; Common Femoral). Code 35301 is used for the same procedure, but for the carotid artery. Code 35302 is also used for the same procedure, but for the superficial femoral artery. Code 35355 is used for the iliofemoral artery.

4. Answer: B – The correct code for the collection of the blood is 36415 (Collection of Venous Blood by Venipuncture). This code is used when a nurse performs the venipuncture in the office, for the purposes of collecting a blood sample. Code 36416 refers to a capillary blood sample that is obtained from the tip of the finger or heel of an infant. Codes 36406 and 36410 are used for the collection of blood when it necessitates the skill of a physician not a nurse.

5. Answer: A – The correct procedure code for the service is 38115 (Repair of Ruptured Spleen (Splenorrhaphy) with or without Partial Splenectomy). It is not necessary to code for 38101 for the partial splenectomy, as the code 38115 includes partial splenectomy as well as the splenorrhaphy. Code 38120 is for a laparoscopic surgical procedure, which is inappropriate.

6. Answer: D – The appropriate codes for the service are 38200 (Injection Procedure for Splenoportography) and 75810 (Splenoportography, Radiological Supervision and Interpretation). The modifier –26 does not need to be included on the claim because the code for 75810already includes the supervision and interpretation component.

7. Answer: B – The correct code for the procedure performed by the physician is 38220 (Bone Marrow; Aspiration Only). This is the appropriate code because the physician was not harvesting the marrow from the donor. Harvesting codes, such as 38230 and 38232 are only used when the bone marrow is harvested in large amounts in order to transplant the marrow into the patient. In this case, the physician was only aspirating a small sample to test (to see if the donor and the patient were matches).

8. Answer: C – The correct code for the procedure is 38525 (Biopsy or Excision of Lymph Node(s); Open, Deep Axillary Nodes). This code does not need to be reported with more than one unit because the code description allows for the excision of multiple nodes. Code 38555 is also incorrect because this code is used for the excision of a cystic hygroma, not a deep axillary lymph node.

9. Answer: D – The correct code for the procedure is 38792 (Injection Procedure; Radioactive Tracer for Identification of Sentinel Node) which is the primary procedure. Code 75801 (Lymphangiography, Extremity Only, Bilateral, Radiological Supervision and Interpretation) also needs to be reported to indicate the radiological guidance for the lymphangiography procedure. The procedure is not indicated as a bilateral procedure, which would exclude code 75803, which is a bilateral procedure and modifier –50, which indicates that the procedure was bilateral.

10. Answer: A – The correct CPT code is 39561 (Resection, Diaphragm; with Complex Repair).The physician utilized an autogenous free muscle flap, therefore the repair is considered complex. If the physician had only sutured the wound, then the appropriate code would have been 39560 (Resection, Diaphragm; with Simple Repair).

1. Answer: B - Code 40819 Code 40820 is the code for excision or destruction of the frenum. Code 40806 is the code for incision of the labial frenum. Code 40820 is the code for destruction of lesions or scars in the vestibule of the mouth and 40899 is the code for unlisted procedures of the vestibule of the mouth.

2. Answer: B - 41251 is the correct code because this is for a laceration less than 2.5 cm and involves the posterior tongue. Code 41250 is incorrect because it involves the anterior tongue. Code 41252 is incorrect because the laceration is not more than 2.6 cm or complex. Code 41599 is incorrect because there is a listed code that works for this procedure.

3. Answer: A - 41100 code is the only code for biopsy of the tongue involving the anterior two-thirds of the tongue. Code 41105 is incorrect because it is for biopsy of the posterior one-third of the tongue. Code 41108 is incorrect because this is for a biopsy of the floor of the mouth. Code 41112 is incorrect because this is for excision of the lesion with closure of the anterior two-thirds of the tongue and this procedure was only for a biopsy.

4. Answer: C - 42100 is the correct code for uvula biopsy. Code 42000 is incorrect because there was no drainage of an abscess performed. Code 42104 is incorrect because there was no excision of a lesion performed. Code 42140 is incorrect because there was n

5. Answer: A - 42200 is correct because this code for a palatoplasty of the soft and/or hard palates only. Code 42205 is incorrect because there was no closure of the alveolar ridge. Code 42210 is incorrect because there was no bone graft of the alveolar ridge. Code 42215 is incorrect because there was no major revision performed.

6. Answer: A - 42000 is the correct code for drainage of an abscess of the palate or uvula. Code 42100 is incorrect because this code is for a biopsy of the palate or uvula. Code 42104 is incorrect because this is for excision of a lesion and 42140 is incorrect because this code is for auvulectomy.

7. Answer: B - 42305 is the correct code for complicated abscess drainage of the parotid gland. Code 42300 is incorrect because this is for a simple drainage of parotid gland abscess. Code 42310 is incorrect because this is for an intraoral drainage of an abscess in the submaxillary or sublingual glands. Code 42320 is incorrect because this is for the external drainage of an abscess in the submaxillary gland.

8. Answer: C - 42408 is the correct code for excision of a sublingual salivary cyst. Code 42400 is incorrect because this code is for a needle biopsy of the salivary gland. Code 42405 is incorrect because this is for an incisional biopsy of the salivary gland. Code 42409 is incorrect because this is for marsupialization for the sublingual salivary cyst and not for the removal of this cyst.

9. Answer: C - 42820 is the correct code for a tonsillectomy and adenoidectomy for a patient younger than age 12. Code 42825 is incorrect because this code is just for a tonsillectomy. Code 42830 is incorrect because this code is just for an adenoidectomy. Code 42821 is incorrect because this is for a tonsillectomy and adenoidectomy for a patient age 12 or over.

10. Answer: D - 42870 is correct because this code is for the excision or destruction of the lingual tonsil. Code 42825 is incorrect because this code is for tonsillectomy for patient under the age of 12. Code 42826 is incorrect because this code is for tonsillectomy for a patient age 12 or over. Code 42860 is incorrect because this code is for excision of tonsil tags.

50,000 Series CPT®

1. Answer: C - The correct code for the circumcision is 54150 (Circumcision, Using Clamp or Other Device with Regional Dorsal penile or Ring Block). Code 54160 is not correct because it is used for a circumcision without using a clamp or other device. You should not use modifier -47 (Anesthesia by Physician) because the anesthesia was included in the procedure description. Modifier -47 guidelines state that the modifier is not to be used with local anesthesia and a penile ring block is a local anesthetic.

2. Answer: D - The correct code for this procedure is with code 54640 (Orchiopexy, Inguinal Approach, with or without Hernia Repair). Codes 54690 and 54692 are orchiopexy and orchiectomy codes, but are not appropriate because the procedure was not performed laparoscopically. Code 54650 is also incorrect because it is used for an orchiopexy performed via an abdominal approach not an inguinal approach.

3. Answer: A - The correct code for this procedure is 55250 (Vasectomy, Unilateral or Bilateral (Separate Procedure), Including Postoperative Semen Examination(s)). This code does not need to be appended with modifier -50. Modifier -50indicates that the procedure was performed bilaterally. In other words, code 55250 indicates that the procedure performed either unilaterally or bilaterally. Code 55200 is also incorrect because it is used for a vasotomy not the excision of the vas deferens (a vasectomy).

4. Answer: B - The correct code for this surgical procedure is 52601 (Transurethral Electrosurgical Resection of the Prostate Including Control of Postoperative Bleeding, Complete). The procedure TURP stands for transurethral resection of the prostate, which is the procedure described in the procedural note. Code 52500 is only used for the resection of a bladder neck not the prostate. Code 52630 is used for the regrowth of prostatic tissue and modifier-58 is inappropriate because it is used for the primary procedure.

5. Answer: C - Code 56440 would represent the physician's work. Code 56440 (Marsupialization of Bartholin's Gland Cyst) is the correct code because the physician did not simply perform an incision and drainage (which would be reportable with code 56420), but sutured the sides of the cyst to leave it open for drainage. This describes a marsupialization procedure.

6. Answer: D - The correct code for the procedure would be 57425 (Laparoscopy, Surgical, Colpopexy (Suspension of Vaginal Apex). The other codes are also used for a colpopexy, but they are used for procedures performed via an open approach. This procedure states that it was performed with a laparoscope; therefore the laparoscopic procedure is the most appropriate code.

7. Answer: C-The OB should code for this surgical procedure with code 59135 (Surgical Treatment of Ectopic Pregnancy; Interstitial, Uterine Pregnancy Requiring Total Hysterectomy). Code 58150 is inappropriate because it is used for a total hysterectomy performed, for other reasons, not for an ectopic pregnancy. Code 59120 is also inappropriate because it is used for the removal of an ectopic pregnancy located on the fallopian tube or ovary, not in the uterus. Code 59136 codes for the removal of an interstitial uterine pregnancy, but it does not take into account the resection of the uterus.

8. Answer: A - The physician in Atlanta should code for his services with code 59426 (Antepartum Care Only, 7 or More Visits).The patient only saw her Atlanta physician 9 times, therefore the Atlanta physician can only code for the antepartum care that he provided. Code 59425 is only 4-6 antepartum visits. Codes 59410 and 59430 are also incorrect because they refer to postpartum care, which in this case, was provided by the physician in Albuquerque.

9. Answer: C - The correct code is 59001, for the therapeutic amniocentesis with amniotic fluid reduction. Code 76946, for the ultrasonic guidance, would not have to be reported, as it is included as part of code 59001. You should only use 76946 for a diagnostic amniocentesis, which in this case, is incorrect. The withdrawal of the amniotic fluid is a therapeutic procedure.

10. Answer: D–The OB should report code 59610 (Routine Obstetric Care Including Antepartum Care, Vaginal Delivery and Postpartum Care, after Previous Cesarean Delivery). Even though the patient's first child was born vaginally, her second child was delivered by a cesarean section. This type of delivery is referred to as a vaginal birth after cesarean (VBAC).

60,000 Series CPT®

1. Answer: B – 62270 is the correct code for a diagnostic lumbar spinal puncture. Code 62269 is incorrect because this is the code for a biopsy of the spinal cord with a percutaneous needle. Code 62272 is incorrect because this is the code for a therapeutic spinal puncture for drainage of cerebrospinal fluid by needle or by catheter. Code 62273 is incorrect because this code is for the injection/epidural of blood or clot patch.

2. Answer: C – 63005 is the correct code for lumbar laminectomy except when done for spondylolisthesis. Code 63001 is incorrect because this code is for cervical laminectomy. Code 63003 is incorrect because this is for thoracic laminectomy and code 63011 is incorrect because it is for sacral laminectomy.

3. Answer: B – 64553 is the correct code for a percutaneous implantation of a cranial nerve neurostimulator electrode array. Code 64550 is incorrect because this code is for the application of a surface or transcutaneous neurostimulator. Code 64555 is incorrect because this code is for a peripheral nerve and 64561 is incorrect because this code is used for the sacral nerve.

4. Answer: A – 64400 is the correct code for an aesthetic agent injection into the trigeminal nerve, also known as a trigeminal nerve block. Code 64402 is incorrect because this code is for the injection of a facial nerve. Code 64405 is incorrect because this code is for the greater occipital nerve and 64408 is incorrect because this code is for the vagus nerve.

5. Answer: C – 64740 is the correct code for transection or avulsion of the lingual nerve. Code 64732 is incorrect because this is the transection or avulsion of the supraorbital nerve. Code 64734 is incorrect because this code is for the infraorbital nerve and 64742 is incorrect because this code is for the transection or avulsion of the facial nerve.

6. Answer: D – 64712 is the correct code for a neuroplasty of the sciatic nerve. Code 64702 is incorrect because this code is for a digital neuroplasty and 64704 is incorrect because this code is for a neuroplasty of a nerve in the hand or foot. Code 64708 is incorrect because this is for a neuroplasty of a major peripheral nerve of the arm or leg.

7. Answer: B – 64447 is the correct code for a single femoral nerve anesthetic agent injection, also known as a nerve block. Code 64445 is incorrect because this code is for the sciatic nerve and code 64449 is incorrect because this code is for the lumbar plexus nerve. Code 64450 is incorrect because this is for "other" peripheral nerve or branch anesthetic agent injection.

8. Answer: C – 64517 is the correct code for anesthetic agent injection of the superior hypogastric plexus. Code 64505 is incorrect because this injection is for the sphenopalatine ganglion. Code 64510 is incorrect because this code is for injection of the stellate ganglion. Code 64520 is incorrect because this code is for injection of the lumbar or thoracic nerves.

9. Answer: C – 64680 is the correct code for destruction of the celiac plexus nerve by neurolytic agent with or without radiologic monitoring. Code 64646 is incorrect because this code is for the chemodenervation of trunk muscles. Code 64650 is incorrect because this code is for the chemodenervation of eccrine glands. Code 64681 is incorrect because this is the code for the destruction of the superior hypogastric plexus.

10. Answer: B – 64760 is the correct code for the transection of the vagus nerve (vagotomy) using an abdominal approach. Code 64755 is incorrect because this is the code for transection of the vagus nerves limited to the proximal stomach. Codes 64763 and 64766 are both incorrect because these codes involve the transection of the obturator nerves.

Anatomy

1. Answer: C – The patient's level of injury is at the thoracic level, which is in the middle of the back. This is indicated by his ability to move his arms, but not his legs. If it was in the cervical area he would be paralyzed from the neck down and would not be able to move his arms. If it was in the lumbar area he would still be able to move his arms, but not his legs because his injury would be lower than the chest area.

2. Answer: B – The tympanic membrane is often referred to as the ear drum. Taste buds are on the tongue and have nothing to do with the auditory system. The stirrup or stapes is a small bone in the middle ear and the inner ear is the internal part of the auditory system.

3. Answer: D – A nasal polyp can obstruct the nasal passageway making it difficult to breathe. If this is the case, surgical removal of the nasal polyps may be necessary. They are normally benignant generally do not cause cancer in the patient. In addition, they are not large enough to change the shape of the nose or release histamines that cause allergic reactions, although they can develop as a result of chronic inflammation.

4. Answer: B–The term "peripheral" refers to the extremities, so the type of cyanosis that presents on the fingers and toes is peripheral cyanosis. Central cyanosis refers to the center of the body or the torso. Medial cyanosis refers to the midline of the body. Embolic cyanosis refers to cyanosis caused by a blocked blood vessel, not an area of the body.

5. Answer: B – The term "alopecia" is commonly referred to as hair loss. Alopecia can be acute or chronic, resulting in baldness. It can be an inherited trait but can also be the result of chemotherapy, a hormonal imbalance, infections, severe stress, medication side-effect.

6. Answer: A – When a doctor manipulates a dislocated joint back into place he reduces the subluxation. A subluxation is a joint dislocation and the manipulation of a joint back into place is commonly referred to as a reduction.

7. Answer: B – The difference between a craniotomy and a craniectomy is that a craniotomy temporarily removes part of the patient's skull to allow access inside the skull or brain during the procedure. The skull is then replaced once the procedure is completed, while a craniectomy removes a part of the patient's skull and does not replace it once the procedure is completed.

8. Answer: A – If a doctor performed only the antepartum portion of a patient's obstetrical care, she provided services to the patient before she delivered the baby. Antepartum means before delivery. Postpartum refers to the period after delivery.

9. Answer: B – If a patient is in the prone position, he is lying flat on his stomach. If the patient lies flat on his back he is in the supine position. If the patient lies flat on his back with his feet elevated he is in the Trendelenburg position. If the patient is sitting up straight he is in the Fowler's position.

10. Answer: D – The superior eyelid is also referred to as the upper eyelid. The term "superior" means "up" or "above" and so the superior eyelid would be the eyelid on the top. The "inferior" eyelid would be the one on the bottom.

Anesthesia

1. Answer: D - The correct code for the procedure is 01490, (Anesthesia for lower leg cast application, removal, or repair). The patient received anesthesia for the cast application, which was only administered in the lower leg. There were no other anesthesia services provided.

2. Answer: C - The correct codes are 00192 (Anesthesia for procedures on facial bones or skull; radical surgery), 99135, (Anesthesia complicated by utilization of controlled hypotension), and 99100, (Anesthesia for patient of extreme age, younger than 1 year or older than 70). 00211 (Anesthesia for intracranial procedures; craniotomy or craniectomy for evacuation of hematoma) is not appropriate, in this case, because the craniectomy was not performed as a result of a hematoma. Also, because both qualifying circumstances codes apply, both of them must be appended to the anesthesia code.

3. Answer: C - Time starts when the anesthesiologist is present when he/she begins to prepare the patient for induction of anesthesia in the operating room (or equivalent area) and ends when the anesthesiologist is no longer in personal attendance. Answer A is incorrect because the anesthesiologist wasn't present when the time first began and ended at the end of surgery, not at the end of the anesthesiologist's attendance. Answer B is incorrect because the time ended at the surgery end time and not at the end of the anesthesiologist's attendance. Answer D is incorrect because the time started before the anesthesiologist was in attendance.

4. Answer: B- 00834 is the correct code for a hernia repair in the lower abdomen for a child younger than one year of age. 99100 is a correct add on code for patients of extreme age (younger than one year and older than 70). Code 99140 is a correct add on code for a procedure complicated by emergency conditions, such as significant hypotension. Code 99135 is an incorrect add-on code because this code is for anesthesia complicated by utilization of controlled hypotension.

5. Answer: C - 00567 is the correct code for coronary artery bypass grafting (CABG) with pump oxygenator. Code 99116 is the correct add-on code for anesthesia complicated by the utilization of total body hypothermia. Code 00566 is incorrect because this code is for CABG without pump oxygenator. Code 99135 is an incorrect add-on code because this is the code for anesthesia complicated by the utilization of controlled hypotension.

6. Answer: D - The anesthesia service that should have been reported is 01990-P6, (Physiological support for harvesting or organ(s) from brain-dead patient). Modifier -P6 also should have been reported to indicate that the patient's physical status, which in this case, is a declared brain-dead patient whose organs were being removed for donor purposes.

7. Answer: C - The correct anesthesia code is 01214, (Anesthesia for arthroscopic procedures of hip joint; total hip arthroplasty only). Anesthesia guidelines state that when multiple surgical procedures are performed during a single anesthetic administration, the anesthesia code representing the most complex procedure is reported. In this case, the hip arthroplasty is the most complex procedure, which makes 01214 the only code that should be reported.

8. Answer: C - The correct codes are 01952, (Anesthesia for second and third-degree burn excisions or debridement, with or without skin grafting, any site, between 4% and 9% of total body surface area), which accounts for the first 9% of burned area and 01953, (Anesthesia for second and third-degree burn excisions or debridement, with or without skin grafting, any site, each additional 9% total body surface area or part thereof),which accounts for the remaining 4%. The code 99100, (Anesthesia for patient of extreme age, younger than 1 year and older than 70) also needs to be reported to account for the patient's advanced age.

9. Answer: B - The correct code is 92225-47, (Ophthalmoscopy, extended, with retinal drawing, with interpretation and report). Modifier -47, (Anesthesia by Surgeon) must be appended to indicate that the anesthesia service was performed by the physician performing the procedure. According to modifier guidelines, modifier -47 is not to be used on the anesthesia procedure code, but rather appended to the basic service code which in this case is 92225. The anesthesia service code, 00148, should not be reported.

10. Answer: C - The correct code is 00792, (Anesthesia for intra-peritoneal procedures in upper abdomen including laparoscopy; partial hepatectomy or management of liver hemorrhage) and the correct physical status modifier is -P5, which indicates that the patient is in a moribund state and not expected to live without the procedure. The tibia manipulation and percutaneous fixation should not be reported separately because it is considered a minor anesthetic procedure in comparison to the management of the liver hemorrhage.

12-16-20 60%
3-30-21 70%

Coding Guidelines

1. Answer: D - Modifier-32 is the appropriate modifier to use on the claim. Modifier-32, mandated services, is used when a procedure is performed because an official body such as a car or life insurance agency, requests it. Modifier-22 is appropriate for a unusual procedural service, Modifier-51 is used for multiple procedures, and Modifier-99 is used for multiple modifiers.

2. Answer: A - The modifier that you would use to indicate that they were two separate procedures performed on the same date of service would be -59 (Distinct Procedural Service). In the description of modifier -59, it states that it is used to report two services that were performed on "different site or organ system[s]," and as such, it is used to report a repair done on the same date, on two separate body areas (the scalp and arm).

3. Answer: B - Modifier -90 (Outside Laboratory)is the appropriate modifier in this case. Modifier -90 is used when the physician's office bills for the laboratory service, even though they sent the lab sample to an outside laboratory. When the insurance company pays the physician for the lab sample, the physician's office reimburses the lab for the cost of the service.

4. Answer: B- - The two most common modifiers used in radiological services are -TC and -26. Modifier -TC is used to indicate that only the technical component of the service was performed. The technical component is used to bill for both the radiology technician's services and the machine. Modifier -26 is used to indicate professional radiological services (radiological supervision and interpretation). This modifier indicates that the physician is billing for reading the image and interpreting the results not for taking the image.

5. Answer: C - The organizations that approved the ICD-10-CM guidelines and who make up the Cooperating Parties are the American Hospital Association (AHA), American Health Information Management Association (AHIMA), Centers for Medicare & Medicaid Services (CMS), and the National Center for Health Statistics (NCHS). The ICD-10-CM is based on the ICD-10, which is the statistical classification of disease that is published by the World Health Organization. The U.S. Federal Governments Department of Health and Human Services is mentioned in the official guidelines because two of its departments (CMS and NCHS) are part of the organizations that make up the Cooperating Parties for the ICD-10-CM.

6. Answer: A - The proper way to locate a code in the ICD-10-CM is to locate the code in the Alphabetic Index then flip to the Tabular List to identify any guided notations. It is essential to use both of these when locating a code. The Alphabetic Index alone will not always give full code information and may leave out certain notations that are required for the code to be complete. The Tabular List is identified easily by locating the right code in the Alphabetic Index. Both need to be used to locate a code.

7. Answer: B - Laterality is specified in the ICD-10-CM codes. Some codes have "right," "left," and "bilateral" options listed. Other codes do not have "bilateral" listed as an option, in which case you would use both the "left" and "right" codes individually to stipulate bilateral diagnoses. These codes can only be used if the laterality is mentioned in the medical record.

8. Answer: C - Both sign/symptom and unspecified codes are appropriate to use when the actual diagnosis is unable to be made. In some cases, the infecting organism needs to be identified for a specific code to be used, so in these cases when the infecting organism isn't known at the time of the patient's encounter an "unspecified" code is appropriate to be used. ICD-10-CM does have codes for signs and symptoms or "unspecified" codes. Although they are not listed for every possible diagnosis, if they are an option they are allowed to be used based on the information available at the time of the patient's visit/encounter.

9. Answer: D - Sequela or "late effects" are considered the conditions or residual effects after the acute phase of the illness or injury has ended. There is no time limit. It could occur months or years after the initial encounter.

10. Answer: B – The respiratory system subsection in the CPT manual contains, but is not limited to, the nose, accessory sinuses, and trachea/bronchi. Procedure codes for the mouth, throat, and stomach are located in the digestive system subsection, while procedure codes for the heart are located in the cardiovascular system subsection.

Compliance and Regulatory

1. Answer: A - HIPAA stands for Health Insurance Portability and Accountability Act. HIPAA is an Act of Congress, not an association or organization. Those that do not follow HIPAA requirements can be prosecuted. HIPAA also joins with other organizations to ensure that everyone involved in patient healthcare follow its stipulations.

2. Answer: B - The purpose of provider credentialing is to make sure that your provider is correctly licensed to perform procedures. In the credentialing process, insurance companies check a provider's credentials, to make sure he is legal and valid. This process is required as part of the provider's contract with the insurance company.

3. Answer: A - In the RBRVS calculation, the GPCI takes into account the geographic location of a practice or provider. GPCI stands for Geographic Practice Cost Index, and it takes into account the relative price differences in geographical location. The GPCI is a part of the RBRVS (Resource Based Relative Value Scale), which calculates a reasonable fee for procedures.

4. Answer: C - The proper way to code is to identify the reason for the encounter using the documentation for support. Then to consult the Alphabetic Index, review stipulations for modifiers, and confirm with the Tabular List. Using the Tabular List, specificity can be coded at its highest level, based on documentation. Assign the code, making sure that the sequence is correct before submitting to the insurances. Always remember to consult the Alphabetic List, reading all options, cross references, abbreviations, and/or modifiers before moving onto the Tabular List. The Tabular List will allow the highest specificity by referring to the number of characters required in the code and prompting this change before sequencing and submitting to the insurance company for payment.

5. Answer: A - Medically Unlikely Edits (MUEs) are considered to be units of service edits created by CMS to lower the Medicare Fee-For-Service Paid Claims Error Rate.

6. Answer: D - "Place of service" reporting refers to the location of the setting where the patient is treated or the service is provided. Evaluation and management codes can be specific to the setting in which the patient is seen. Certain procedures or services may be specific to a setting, such as therapeutic, diagnostic or prophylactic. Facilities may also be specified whether in the hospital, at home, in a physician's office or in a nursing home. Whatever location in which the encounter occurs is the "place of service."

7. Answer: C - Both A and B are correct. Services provided within the home by someone part of an agency are considered facility services. Services provided by a physician or provider who is not part of an agency are not facility services, they are termed "non-facility" services.

8. Answer: B - The CPT guidelines specify that terms such as "physician," "qualified healthcare professional," and "individual" are not used to exclude, instead it is meant that other entities besides those specific ones can report services too, unless specifically stipulated in a procedural guideline.

9. Answer: A - This is a federal law that prevents fraud and abuse from happening when one provider may refer to another specific provider and when that provider would then benefit from anything of value. Physicians are not allowed to accept money or other payment of value for recruitment or referrals of patients. The law doesn't protect providers from being charged with a felony when this happens; instead it specifies the fines associated with this felony. It doesn't protect patients from being referred out, only from physician's receiving a kickback from the referral.

10. Answer: B - These edits are updated quarterly and can be found on the CMS website. The NCCI Edit Tables are updated quarterly, not monthly, semi-annually or annually.

Evaluation and Management

1. Answer: D - You would report this office visit with the E&M codes: 99215 (Established Patient Office Visit, Level Five), and 99354 and 99355 (X2) (Prolonged Services). Code 99215 is established by the detailed history, comprehensive examination, and the MDM of high complexity. The appropriate prolonged services codes are: 99354 (First 30-74 minutes Over), which represents the time spent beyond what is allowed for the 99215 code and the 99355 (X2) (Rest of the Time Spent with the Patient), which in this case is a total of 1 hour and 45 minutes. If the physician spent 1 hour and 44 minutes, then the correct number of units for 99355 would be 1, but that is not the case.

2. Answer: C - You should code this service using information from the evaluation and management chapter of the CPT manual. A pelvic examination without anesthesia should be coded as part of the regular evaluation and management service. This information can be found in the evaluation and management chapter. If the patient needed a pelvic examination under general anesthesia, it should be coded as a service greater than an E&M service and reported using code 57410.

3. Answer: B - The OB/GYN should code for this visit with 99395 (Routine Physical and Pelvic Examination). OB/GYNs are considered primary care physicians who can perform routine physical examinations. Code 57170 (Diaphragm or Cervical Cap Fitting with Instructions) also needs to be included on the claim because the OB performed an additional service. Furthermore, it is necessary to combine the modifier -59 with code 57170 to indicate that there was a distinct procedural service provided to the patient on the same day as an E/M service, which in this case, is a routine physical and pelvic exam.

4. Answer: B - The correct E&M code is 99386 (Periodic Comprehensive Preventive Medicine, New Patient, 40-64 Years of Age). The patient is new to the physician, so the codes: 99396 and 99397 are incorrect. 99396 and 99397 are used for established patients. Furthermore, code 99387 is used for patients at least 65 years old.

5. Answer: B - The E&M service that can be reported for this phone call is 99442 (Telephone E&M Service Provided by a Qualified Non-Physician Health Care Professional; 11-20 Minutes of Medical Discussion). The phone call did not originate from a previous visit (within the last 7 days) and it also did not occur in response to an upcoming doctor's visit (within the next 24 hours), therefore you can code for this service. In addition, code 99442 is more appropriate than 98967 because a nurse practitioner qualifies as a non-physician health care professional.

6. Answer: A - 99218 is the correct code for an initial observation care of low complexity with a detailed history and examination. Code 99219 is incorrect because this code is for medical decision making of moderate complexity. Code 99220 is incorrect because this code is for initial observation care of a patient requiring high complexity medical decision making. Code 99224 is incorrect because this code is for subsequent observation care and not for the initial encounter.

7. Answer: B - 99219 is the correct code for an initial observation care requiring moderate complexity medical decision making. Code 99218 is incorrect because this observation patient required more than low complexity or straightforward medical care. Code 99220 is incorrect because the hospitalist did not spend enough time on the unit with this patient initially and this patient did not require high complexity medical decision making. Code 99224 is incorrect because this code is for subsequent observation care and not the initial care.

8. Answer: D - 99226 is the correct code for subsequent observation care of a patient requiring more than 35 minutes of care requiring high complexity medical decision making with detailed interval history and detailed examination since initial observation care was given. Code 99220 is incorrect because this code is for the initial observation care of a high complexity medical decision making encounter. Code 99224 is incorrect because, while it is the code for a subsequent observation encounter, this is for a patient that is straightforward or of low complexity. Code 99225 is incorrect because

this code is for a patient of moderate complexity typically only requiring 25 minutes of care at the bedside or on the patient's unit.

9. Answer: D - 99239 is the correct code for hospital discharge day management that took more than 30 minutes. Codes 99235 and 99236 are both incorrect because these codes are for observation or inpatient hospital care not involving discharge. Code 99238 is incorrect because this code is for discharge requiring less than 30 minutes of management.

10. Answer: C - 99244 is the correct code for an office consultation involving 60 minutes of care, a comprehensive history and physical examination and medical decision making of moderate complexity. Code 99242 is incorrect because this code is for an office consultation that requires straight forward medical decision making and an expanded problem-focused history and examination. Code 99243 is incorrect because this code is for an office consultation involving a comprehensive history and examination as well as moderate-complexity medical decision making. Code 99245 is incorrect because this office consultation code is for a visit that is usually 80 minutes, requiring high-complexity medical decision making.

HCPCS Level II

1. Answer: A - HCPCS Level II codes are updated every quarter by CMS (Centers for Medicare and Medicaid Services). Updates to HCPCS Level II codes are published on the CMS website at the beginning of each new quarter. The HCPCS Level II manual, however, is only published once per year.

2. Answer: B - Appendix A in the HCPCS Level II manual contains a table of drugs. This table lists all of the drugs in alphabetical order and can be found in the HCPCS manual. The listings are also organized according to the drugs administration route and unit information.

3. Answer: C - The purpose of temporary national codes in the HCPCS Level II manual is to allow the establishment of codes prior to the January 1st annual update. Temporary codes are also developed in order to meet the needs of newly established policies and legal requirements. If the temporary code becomes permanent, it is deleted and becomes a permanent code.

4. Answer: C - J0696 x 2 is the correct code because this code is for Ceftriaxone sodium 250 mg. Because this patient received two times this amount of medication, this code needs to reflect this multiplication. Code J0715 is incorrect because this code is for 500 mg Ceftizoxime sodium. J0696 is incorrect unless doubled, because this code is only for 250 mg of Ceftriaxone sodium. Code J0697 is incorrect because this code is for 750 mg Cefuroxime sodium. All of these codes can be used for IM or IV administration.

5. Answer: C - The HCPCS Level II modifier -E1 stands for Upper Right, Eyelid. Many HCPCS modifiers indicate anatomical locations, such as the -E series modifiers for eyelids. Other HCPCS modifiers indicate a section of the vertebral column, and digits of the hands or feet.

6. Answer: B - The HCPCS manual includes codes for supplies, services, and procedures that are not found in the CPT manual. Although some procedures found in the HCPCS manual are also found in the CPT manual, the most appropriate answer is B because HCPCS codes also include supplies and services not found in the CPT manual.

7. Answer: B - Vision and Hearing services are located in the V0000 through V5999 section of the HCPCS manual. Pathology and Laboratory services are located in the P0000 through P9999 section. Dental Procedures are located in the D0000 through D9999 section. Transportation services are located in the A0000 through A0999 section.

8. Answer: A - The best, most effective way to locate the correct code for a service or supply in the HCPCS manual is to look in the Index for the name of the service or supply, and it will direct you to the correct code or range of codes. Checking the Index first is the most efficient way of locating the correct code because it lists all codes that may be applicable for that service or supply. This way you can check all codes to make sure you assign the correct one.

9. Answer: A - HCPCS J-Codes are used to represent drugs administered by methods other than the oral method. The J-codes are used to bill drugs administered to the patient, while in the office. Other sections in the HCPCS manual represent durable medical equipment and temporary national codes. Dental procedures are not represented at all in the CPT manual, and are reported with D-codes.

10. Answer: A - The abbreviation "VAR" stands for "Various Routes." Other routes of administration include: "IA" for "Intra-arterial," "IM" for "Intra-muscular," "INH" for "Inhalant solution," and "OTH" for "Other routes of administration."

ICD-10-CM

1. Answer: C - A04.7, B20 is the correct answer because code A04.7 is the primary code for enterocolitis due to Clostridium difficile, which is the primary reason for admission. The HIV is subsequent in this particular case because it is not the main reason the patient was being admitted. However, it is still necessary to consider for best plan of care and treatment of the patient. B20 is not the primary code so should not be listed first. R75 is the code for inconclusive serologic evidence of HIV which is incorrect for this patient since this patient has been diagnosed with HIV in the past.

2. Answer: C - D64.81, C91.00, T45.1X5A is the correct code sequence for a patient who was admitted for anemia requiring a blood transfusion due to the chemotherapy, from the treatment he is undergoing for acute lymphoblastic leukemia. The anemia code is the primary code and is specific to the chemotherapy. The secondary code is the type of leukemia that he has; he is currently undergoing treatment, so he is not in remission. The last code is for an adverse effect of antineoplastic and immunosuppressive drugs, initial encounter. C91.10 is incorrect because this is not the right code for acute lymphoblastic leukemia.

3. Answer: A- E10.10 is the correct code for Type 1 diabetes mellitus with ketoacidosis without coma. E10.319 is the correct code for Type 1 diabetes mellitus with unspecified diabetic retinopathy without macular edema. Code Z79.4 is the code used for patients who routinely use insulin and this patient has an insulin pump. Code E10.11 is incorrect because this code is for Type 1 diabetes mellitus with ketoacidosis with coma. Code E10.311 is incorrect because this code is for Type 1 diabetes mellitus with unspecified diabetic retinopathy with macular edema.

4. Answer: B - F33.1, F41.1, F17.210 is the correct ICD code sequence for this patient. F33.1 is the correct code for moderate recurrent major depressive disorder. F41.1 is the correct code for generalized anxiety disorder and F17.210 is the correct code for nicotine dependency by cigarettes without complications. F33.0 is incorrect because this code is for mild recurrent major depressive disorder. F41.9 is incorrect because this code is for unspecified anxiety disorder. F17.200 is incorrect because this code is for unspecified uncomplicated nicotine dependence and this patient's nicotine of choice is cigarettes.

5. Answer: D - G44.229 is the correct code for chronic tension type headache that is not intractable. Code G43.10 is incorrect because this code is for migraine with aura and G44.019 is incorrect because this code is for episodic cluster headaches. Code G44.201 is incorrect because this code is for unspecified tension-type headaches that are intractable.

6. Answer: A - H00.11 is the correct code for a chalazion of the right upper eyelid. Code H00.12 is incorrect because this code is for a chalazion of the right lower eyelid. Code H00.13 is incorrect because this is the code for a chalazion of the right eye without the eyelid specified. Code H00.14 is incorrect because this code is for a chalazion of the left upper eyelid.

7. Answer: C - H65.01, H61.22 is the correct sequence for this patient. H65.01 is the correct code for right acute serous otitis media. H61.22 is the correct code for impacted cerumen in the left ear. Code H65.02 is incorrect because this code is for left acute serous otitis media. Code H65.03 is incorrect as well because this code is for bilateral acute serous otitis media. Code H61.21 is incorrect because this code is for cerumen impaction in the right ear.

8. Answer: D - J45.21, J00 is the correct sequence of codes for this patient because J45.21 is the correct code for mild intermittent asthma with acute exacerbation and J00 is the correct code for acute nasopharyngitis, also known as the common cold. Code J45.20 is incorrect because this code is for uncomplicated mild intermittent asthma. Code J45.31 is incorrect because this code is for mild persistent asthma with acute exacerbation and J22 is incorrect because this code is for unspecified lower respiratory infection.

9. Answer: C - K50.8 is the correct code for Crohn's disease of both small and large intestines without complications. Code K50.0 is incorrect because this code is specific to the small intestine and K50.1 is incorrect because this code is for disease of the large intestine. Code K50.9 is incorrect because this code is for unspecified Crohn's disease.

10. Answer: B – L01.01 is the correct code for non-bullous impetigo. Code L01.00 is incorrect because this is for impetigo that hasn't been specified. Code L01.02 is incorrect because this code is for Bockhart's impetigo, also known as perifolliculitis, and code L01.03 is incorrect because this is for bullous impetigo.

Laboratory/Pathology

1. Answer: D – The surgical pathologist should code for this service using codes 88304 with 3 units, to indicate the sampling of three separate skin tags. Code 88309 with 4 units should be used to indicate the four separate samples of breast tissue. Level VI codes (88309) are more appropriate than Level V codes (88307) because the procedure was a mastectomy with removal of regional lymph nodes. If the procedure had been a partial or simple mastectomy, then code 88307 (Level V) would have been the correct surgical pathology code.

2. Answer: B – 80050 is the correct code for a general health panel and, because the general health panel includes the comprehensive metabolic panel, this panel is not coded in addition to the 80050. Code 80053 is incorrect because this code is for the comprehensive metabolic panel, but because another panel that is more extensive that includes the comprehensive metabolic panel was also ordered, this code overlaps with the general health panel code 80050. Code 80051 is incorrect because this code is for an electrolyte panel, which is part of the comprehensive metabolic panel and part of the general health panel. Code 80048 is also incorrect because this is a basic metabolic panel, which is included within the comprehensive metabolic panel.

3. Answer: A – 80300 is the correct code for direct optical observation drug testing of any number of drug classes from Drug Class A. Because no additional testing was performed, there is no need for additional codes. Code 80301 is incorrect because this is for a single drug class using instrumented tests systems. Code 80302 is incorrect because this code is for Drug Class List B and 80303 is incorrect because this code is used for any number of drug class screens using chromatography procedures and not direct optical observation.

4. Answer: A – 80162 is the correct code for a total Digoxin level. Code 80163 is incorrect because this code is for a free Digoxin level. Code 80159 is incorrect because this code is for the therapeutic drug assay for clozapine and code 80178 is the code for a lithium therapeutic drug assay.

5. Answer: C – 80185 and 80186 are the correct codes for total and free Phenytoin, and code 80201 is the correct code for Topiramate therapeutic drug assay tests. Code 80184 is incorrect because this code is used for the drug Phenobarbital. Code 80183 is incorrect because this code is for the drug Oxcarbazepine and code 80200 is incorrect because this code is for the drug Tobramycin.

Medical Terminology

1. Answer: B – This organ is called the pharynx. The esophagus is the tube that arises from the pharynx, the organ that carries food through the diaphragm into the stomach. The trachea is not a digestive organ; it is the respiratory organ that connects the nose to the mouth and the mouth to the lungs.

2. Answer: A – The condition that occurs when the lining of the esophagus becomes inflamed and is generally caused by an infection or irritation of the esophagus is called esophagitis. In medical terminology, the suffix "itis" means inflammation so esophagitis literally means "inflammation of the esophagus."

3. Answer: C – A dilated and enlarged varicose vein that developed inside the rectum and slipped outside of the anus is called a prolapsed hemorrhoid. An external hemorrhoid is one that occurs on the outside of the rectum, while an internal hemorrhoid is one that occurs inside the rectum and is still inside the rectum. A prolapsed hemorrhoid has slipped from the inside of the rectum to the outside.

4. Answer: A – The pair of tubular glands located above the prostate and behind the bladder that lubricate the duct system, nourish the sperm, and contribute fluid to the ejaculate is called seminal vesicles. The testes produce and store sperm cells. The vas deferens transports semen from the epididymis to the pelvis. The epididymis is a coiled tube that connects the testicles to the vas deferens.

5. Answer: B – One of the most common prostatic disorders is benign prostatic hyperplasia (BPH), which is an enlargement of the prostate gland. This disorder may require a transurethral resection of the prostate (TURP).Benign prostatic hyperplasia is caused by the excessive growth of prostatic nodules. BPH can compress the urethra, leading to partial or complete obstruction of the urethra, urinary hesitancy, frequency, dysuria, urinary retention and an increased risk of urinary tract infections.

Medicine

1. Answer: D - You would code this procedure with 69930-50 (Bilateral Cochlea Device Implantation, With or Without Mastoidectomy).You would use this code because it refers to the cochlear device implantation procedure and it includes the mastoidectomy. The two procedures do not need to be reported separately. Code 69900 also needs to be included on the report to indicate that the physician used an operating microscope to aid in the procedure.

2. Answer: C - The correct code for the cardiologist's office is 93041 (Rhythm ECG, 1-3; Tracing Only Without Interpretation and Report).The interpretation of the ECG was performed by the patient's primary care physician, therefore the cardiologist can only bill for the technical component of the ECG, which in this case is the tracing only. The primary care physician's office, on the other hand, can only bill for the interpretation of the report, because the PCP only interpreted the test results and diagnosed the patient.

3. Answer: D - The electrocardiogram should be reported with the code 93040 (Rhythm ECG, 1-3 Leads; with Interpretation and Report). Codes 93000 and 93010 should not be reported because the ECG was a rhythm ECG, not a routine ECG. Code 93042 (Rhythm ECG, 1-3 Leads; Interpretation and Report Only) also should not be reported because the physician performed the ECG, interpreted and reported the results of the ECG, instead of just interpreting the results.

4. Answer: D - The correct code for this service is 93288 (Interrogation Device Evaluation with Analysis Review and Report; Single, Dual, or Multiple Lead Pacemaker System).Code 33208 is used for the actual insertion of the pacemaker, while code 33213 is used for the insertion of pacemaker pulse generator only. Code 93289 is used for the analysis of a cardioverter-defibrillator system not a pacemaker system.

5. Answer: C - The correct codes for this service are 93453 (Combined Right and Left Heart Catheterization including Intraprocedural Injections(s) for Left Ventriculography, Imaging Supervision and Interpretation, when Performed) and 93464 (Physiologic Exercise Study (e.g. Bicycle or Arm Ergometry).Code 93531 is only reported when the combined catheterization is performed for congenital cardiac anomalies and codes 93451 and 93452 are only used for either a right or left heart catheterization.

Radiology

1. Answer: B - 76825 is the correct code for fetal echocardiography in real time with image documentation (2D) with M-mode recording. Code 76820 is incorrect because this code is for fetal Doppler velocimetry. Code 76826 is incorrect because this code is for a follow-up or repeat fetal echocardiogram and code 76827 is incorrect because this code is for fetal Doppler echocardiography with pulsed wave and/or continuous wave with spectral display.

2. Answer: B - 77003 is the correct code for fluoroscopic guidance and localization of needle or catheter tip for spine or paraspinous diagnostic or therapeutic injection procedures (epidural or subarachnoid). Code 77002 is incorrect because this code is for fluoroscopic guidance for needle placement (biopsy, aspiration, injection, localization device). Code 77011 is incorrect because this code is for computed tomography guidance for stereotactic localization. Code 77012 is incorrect because this code is for computed tomography guidance for needle placement, radiological supervision and interpretation.

3. Answer: C - 77021 is the correct code for magnetic resonance guidance for needle placement (e.g., for biopsy, needle aspiration, injection, or placement of localization device) radiological supervision and interpretation. Codes 77011 and 77012 are incorrect because these codes are for computed tomography guidance procedures. Code 77022 is incorrect because this code is for magnetic resonance guidance for, and monitoring of, parenchymal tissue ablation.

4. Answer: B - 77002 is the correct code for fluoroscopic guidance for needle placement (e.g., biopsy, aspiration, injection, localization device). Code 77001 is incorrect as this is an add-on code for fluoroscopic guidance for central venous access device placement. Code 77003 is incorrect because this code is for fluoroscopic guidance and localization of needle or catheter tip for spine or paraspinous diagnostic or therapeutic injection procedures. Code 77011 is incorrect because this code is for computed tomography guidance for stereotactic localization.

5. Answer: D - 77057, 77052 is the correct code sequence for this procedure. 77057 is the correct code for a screening mammography, bilateral with 2-view film study of each breast and 77052 is the correct code for computer-aided detection during a screening mammography. Code 77054 is incorrect because this code is for a mammary ductogram or galactogram. Code 77056 is incorrect because this is for a bilateral mammography, but not for a screening mammography. Code 77057 is correct, but alone does not include computer-aided detection and requires the additional code to indicate this further testing.

Made in the USA
Columbia, SC
12 March 2018